The Cross

The Cross

Its Meaning and Message in a Postmodern World

DOUGLAS VICKERS

WIPF & STOCK · Eugene, Oregon

THE CROSS
Its Meaning and Message in a Postmodern World

Copyright © 2010 Douglas Vickers. All rights reserved. Except for brief quotations in critical publications or reviews, no part of this book may be reproduced in any manner without prior written permission from the publisher. Write: Permissions, Wipf and Stock Publishers, 199 W. 8th Ave., Suite 3, Eugene, OR 97401.

Wipf & Stock
An Imprint of Wipf and Stock Publishers
199 W. 8th Ave., Suite 3
Eugene, OR 97401
www.wipfandstock.com

ISBN 13: 978-1-60899-429-8

Manufactured in the U.S.A.

Scripture quotations, unless otherwise stated, are from the King James Version

Contents

Preface vii

1 Preliminary Issues 1

2 Biblical Foundations 27

3 The Cross: Its Meaning and Message 54

4 Justification and the Christian Life 77

5 The Refuge of the Cross 102

6 The Sufficiency of the Cross 121

7 Biblical Inspiration and Authority 134

Bibliography 157

Preface

MY OBJECTIVE IN THIS book is to suggest a number of aspects from which the cross and the redemptive work of Christ are to be viewed. In the opening chapter I have commented briefly on several questions that provide the context in which the following chapters are developed. A principal question that calls for preliminary comment is what I refer to as the human condition to which the cross is addressed. That is a condition of sin and estrangement from God by reason of the bequest of Adam's fall. But the human condition, which has taken on particular characteristics under the influence of the history of thought, exhibits at this time the multiform features of what has been referred to as postmodernism. I return to some aspects of that contemporary movement in chapter 5. Chapter 1 reflects also on the being and holiness of God that lies behind the provision of the cross, and on the terms of the Covenant of Grace of which the cross of Christ is the culminating effect.

The meaning of the cross, taking up the important questions of who it was who went to the cross, why the cross was necessary in the divine purpose, and the benefits that accrue to those who were the subjects of the redemption the cross provided, is addressed directly in chapter 3. Prior to that, and to anticipate the principal questions involved, chapter 2 adduces aspects of the biblical revelation that provides the explanation of the cross. The scripturicity of the Scriptures has come under attack in recent times, even within the Reformed-evangelical church, and I have therefore included in the final chapter a slightly fuller discussion of the inspiration and reliability of the biblical data. At that point also I have commented on some of the contemporary deviations from accepted historical positions.

Chapter 4 takes up a central implication of what had to that point been said regarding the efficacy for salvation of the atonement the cross provided. It brings into conjunction, and recognizes their dependence on the Covenant of Grace, the "accepting, receiving, and resting on Christ alone" as aspects of saving faith and the "justification, sanctification, and eternal life" that follow from the redemptive achievement of the cross.

In chapter 5 the cross is seen as a refuge for the sinner who, by the regenerating grace of God, is made aware of his perilous state in sin, a refuge for the Christian believer who has again fallen into sin, and, of singular importance, a refuge for the Christian who faces and is tortured by the pressure of temptation to sin. Chapter 6 sees in the cross its absolute sufficiency to accomplish all that was intended in the divine Covenant of Redemption, and it returns to the question of the imperatives that are laid on the Christian believer by reason of his redemption that the Christ of the cross has provided.

A note on terminology is in order. Throughout the book I have followed traditional theological usage and employed the nouns "man" and "men" to refer to mankind in general, and my use of the pronoun "he" and its cognates is intended in a generic sense to refer to people inclusively, in a manner that avoids the alternative repetitive use of "his or her."

I acknowledge my heavy indebtedness to a long line of Reformed theologians, to whose work I have endeavored to give credit in the text. Any apparent originality in the arguments I present is due to the impact on my thinking and meditations of those scholars whose insights have had formative influence in the subject areas I have addressed. My professional career has been spent in the professoriate of a non-theological academic discipline. But my understanding of, and appreciation for, Reformed doctrinal and apologetic theology has benefited greatly, as is undoubtedly reflected in this book, from the influence of the scholarship of John Murray and Cornelius Van Til whom I was privileged to know during their tenure at Westminster Theological Seminary, and from the ministry of Martyn Lloyd-Jones at Westminster Chapel while I was completing doctoral studies at the University of London. I acknowledge my indebtedness to them.

I happily record my deep gratitude to the Rev. Al LaValley who read and gave me valuable comments on my draft manuscript, and as has been true for many books and professional papers over the years, to Ann Hopkins for her invaluable editorial assistance. For the blemishes and infelicities that remain in the work I take full responsibility.

1

Preliminary Issues

THE QUESTION THAT HAS challenged the ages remains relentlessly new: How do we explain the presence of Jesus Christ in this world? Souls laden by the search for truth have found relief in the Scriptures' answer, even as many, like a rich young ruler of old, have turned away in incredulity: "Christ Jesus came into the world to save sinners" (1 Tim 1:15). The cross of Christ stands prominently as the watershed of history. All that the providence of God eventuated preceding it finds its explanation and reason for being in the cross. All that has followed in the histories of men and nations has been formed by a divine hand in the realization of the purposes for which the cross occurred. The cross of Christ has been an enigma and offense to those whose assertion of autonomy has stood between them and eternal life, but it has spoken peace and eternal rest to many who, wearied by the burden of sin, have been reconciled to God by the atonement set forth in the cross. All of history, precedent to the cross and following from it, has been eventuated by God in the interests of the church that Christ, by virtue of the cross, redeemed.

Reflect, for a moment, on the apostolic summary of the meaning projected by the death of Christ on the cross: "Whom God hath set forth to be a propitiation [or setting at peace the wrath of God against sin] through faith in his blood, to declare his righteousness for the remission [or pretermission; that is, 'passing over'] of sins that are past [or were committed in former times], through the forbearance of God; To declare, I say, at this time his righteousness: that he might be just, and the justifier of him which believeth in Jesus" (Rom 3:25–26). The point of the statement is that God had in his patience and restraint passed over, or refrained from punishing, sins committed under the earlier administration of the old covenant, but that now he has set forth Christ to be a propitiation for sin. In doing so, God is showing that he is perfectly righteous, because what he is now doing in Christ has reference to all the sin of all his people, both those in the past and now present and those that are still to come. In other words, the sacrifices under the Old Testament Levitical administration could not definitively take away sin. They achieved only a ceremonial cleansing so that those who brought the sacrifice could approach God in worship. But now that Christ as the antitype of the Old Testament priesthood had come in order that he should himself be the final offering for sin, God's justice and righteousness would be completely declared and satisfied. God, then, is just, because he has poured out on his Son on the cross the full extent of his wrath against sin. Sin, the sin of all his people of all time, was dealt with once and for all on the cross.

Because God has punished sin in his Son on the cross he can, as the text says, be just and the justifier of those who believe in Jesus. Martyn Lloyd-Jones has observed that "in many senses there are no more important verses in the whole range and realm of Scripture than these two verses."[1] Here again is the remarkable reality that in the covenantal design of God "Christ died for sinners." The objective was that we to whom the guilt of Adam's transgression had been imputed, who had inherited the fallen nature that resulted from Adam's dereliction, might again be "reconcile[d] . . . unto God . . . by the cross" (Eph 2:16). It was in order that it could then be said that we "through him [Christ] . . . have access by one Spirit unto the Father" (Eph 2:18). In that entrance to the Father by reason of our union with the Christ of the cross, "we have boldness and access with confidence" (Eph 3:12).

Before we look in more detail at the meaning and the message of the cross, it will be useful to consider certain preliminary issues and questions that will provide a context and background for further interpretation. The questions present themselves, first, as to what is the character and nature of the human condition that made the cross necessary; second, what, in the light of that, is to be understood as the purpose of God in the redemption the cross provided; and third, what is to be seen as the thought structures of the world that contend for authentication against the scriptural claims we have already adduced?

---

1. Lloyd-Jones, *The Cross: The Vindication of God*, 1.

THE HUMAN CONDITION

A confluence of cultural and theological concerns engages the Christian mind. In one of its most piercing aspects, the problem of our time is the problem of man himself. The complex pressures of the times have made him unsure of his place in the world and his prospects and destiny. That the entrance of sin has contaminated the whole of life, that it has reduced man to a state of moral inability, and that it alone opens the way to adequate explanation will engage us at length. But what of the condition of man to whom the revivifying word of God comes? On the socio-cultural level the problem is that of modern man enmeshed in a terribly human condition in which the individual has lost a clear view of his status and his place. On the level of theology, or of the doctrinal belief and the relevance of the church, questions press as to what light from Christian perspectives is thrown, or should be thrown, on the issues.

To say, however, that the modern problem is the problem of modern man is to say, in a sense, nothing new. The highly important movement of Renaissance thought in the thirteenth to the fifteenth centuries fostered a humanism that was countered and reshaped in its theological dimension by the Reformation. That latter was primarily a theological movement that bequeathed to the subsequent history of Western civilization social, political, and cultural benefits. The importance of Calvin, for example, at the height of the Reformation, derives from both the theological and the socio-cultural influence of his work. On the level of theological doctrine, Calvin's work was crafted within the context of a consciousness of the sovereignty and covenantal purpose of God. While the genius of his thought derived from his God-consciousness, its significance lay, in an important respect, in the manner in which he responded to the Renaissance recovery of the importance of the individual. For Calvin, that came to expression on two levels. First, he gave to the church not only the importance of the priesthood of Christ within the context of the threefold offices of Christ (as prophet, priest, and king), but in conjunction with that he gave emphasis to the importance of the individual in his doctrine of the universal priesthood of believers.[2] Second, those closely related aspects of his thought imply that he stood for a divine monergism in salvation, against the human autosoterism of

---

2. See Calvin, *Institutes*, 4.18.17, citing 1 Pet 2:9; Heb 13:15.

the Pelagians and the synergism in the semi-Pelagianism of Rome.[3] That implied, in turn, that Calvin clarified the biblical meaning of sin and moral inability to which the redemptive work of Christ was addressed, and against that he clarified and insisted on the reality of the believer's union with Christ. Though Calvin's work spread its influence to the socio-cultural level in its implication, again, of the sanctity of individual freedom, that influence has been tarnished in more modern times by a failure to recognize that sin is abroad in the world and in the hearts of men.

With the birth of modern philosophy in the hands of Descartes in the seventeenth century, his *cogito ergo sum*, I think therefore I am, established a decidedly anthropocentric orientation of thought. That orientation was consolidated in the so-called Enlightenment of the eighteenth century, and at the end of the century the autonomy of man, so far as the philosophy of the possibilities of human thought was concerned, was definitively established by the work of Immanuel Kant. The argument of the ancient Greek philosopher, Protagoras, had come back to vogue, and man was now again "the measure of all things." That orientation has persisted. And in the light of more modern developments it is necessary for the church and its theology to respond to what has become the interpretative and diagnostic bankruptcy of contemporary non-Christian humanism. For the inner logic and the gathering momentum of modern thought has fathered a new humanism that has set the stage for a complete devolution of thought away from its earlier and secure moorings.

---

3. Pelagius was a British monk who claimed that the faculties of the soul had not been subject to depravity as a result of Adam's fall in the manner we shall go on to explore. He argued, as Harnack observes in his *Outlines of the History of Dogma*, 370, that "All men stand in the condition of Adam before his fall." Every person, therefore, "is able to resist every sin [and] he must do so." In his larger work on the *History of Dogma*, 5:175, (quoted in Sproul, *Faith Alone*, 136), Harnack refers to the Pelagian doctrine as stated at the Synod of Carthage in the year 418 as claiming that "man can be without sin and keep the divine commands easily if he will." For Pelagianism in its varying degrees the will is perfectly free to accept or reject the offer of salvation that Christ provided. Effectively, therefore, anyone who is saved is saved by his own decision and choice, and the sovereign grace of God is not necessarily involved in salvation in any prior sense. Man effectively saves himself. That is "autosoterism." In the semi-Pelagianism of Roman Catholic theology, salvation is a matter of cooperation between the grace of God and the freewill choice of the individual person. That is effectively a "synergism." It again diminishes the biblical meaning of the grace of God and robs God of his sovereignty. Salvation, as we shall go on to see, is a "divine monergism"(salvation is due to God alone), not an "autosoterism" or a divine-human "synergism." See a fuller discussion in Vickers, *Divine Redemption*, 10–17.

When it is said that man has made himself "the measure of all things," the import of that is expressed on two levels which, taken together, are correlative to each other. First, on the level of behavior or ethics, man is the measure of all things in that he sets his own standards or criteria of goodness, and in doing so he loses himself in a shoreless ocean of relativism in which his structureless norms have lost all grip on an earlier absoluteness. Second, man has become the measure of all things on the level of the possibility and validity of knowledge. His criteria of truth are excogitated from within himself or are discovered in the fashions of thought that exist in the cultural milieu in which he finds himself. Putting together the modern assertion of autonomy in the areas of behavior and knowledge, man has cut himself off completely from earlier and revelatory moorings. What now impresses the reflective mind as the loss of cultural cohesion in the world and the insecurity if not bankruptcy of theology is the result, on the one hand, of a rampantly apostate view, and on the other of at least a sub-biblical view, of man.

Consider for a moment the biblical doctrine. The authors of the Westminster Confession, the outstanding English expression of Reformed theology in the seventeenth century, wrote into their Shorter Catechism: "God created man . . . after his own image, in knowledge, righteousness, and holiness."[4] We note in the conceptual trilogy implicit in the catechism the point at which biblical anthropology begins: first, God created man; second, God created man in his own image; and third, man as he came from the hands of his Creator existed in a state of knowledge, righteousness, and holiness. We shall return to the sequel, to sin and the fall, and to the towering categories of redemption that followed. But the pressing need at present is not only that of a careful examination of what the trilogy of propositions implies. The question presses as to whether the theology of the church has lost its grip on the doctrinal orientation which such propositions as these provide.

It is undoubtedly true that in a pluralistic society the church, in spite of what might have been the case in earlier centuries, has ceased to be an effective and cementing establishment. In what is now the radical pluralism of society, no single force appears capable of functioning universally as an effective and culturally coordinating element. No single force exerts a predominant, determining influence or a cultural hegemony or leadership except the applied forms of the new humanism,

---

4. Westminster Shorter Catechism, Question 10.

particularly in its scientific and its several empirical expressions. But the issue before us is that for all such reasons, the church and its theology confront a crisis of comprehension in which the very explanation of man stands like a riddle at the core.

What are we to say of the church at this time, of the kaleidoscope of its theologies, its movements to doctrinal ecumenicity, and its turmoil in ecclesiastical forms? Has the church not lost the battle, it is time to ask, or are we not perilously in danger of doing so by falling prey to some of the shallowest fallacies of the age: the fallacies of imagining that we could have an evangelism, or an evangelicalism, without the biblical evangel; that we could be effective preachers of the word of life and not be careful to hold the biblical truths in biblical proportion; that we could bend to the behavior norms of the age and become careless in our handling of holy things; or that, to face the issue on the level of every day, we could imagine the Christian ethic and the wholesomeness of life to be supportable without the Christian doctrine?

THE BIBLICAL RESPONSE

Against the contemporary scene, and in the context of the cultural forces we have noted as bearing on it, the need of the church is to recapture and maintain the biblical doctrine of man and of his sinful fall. That, we have seen, begins with the statement that "God created man." "Let us make man in our image" (Gen 1:26), God said, addressing the Second and Third Persons of the Trinity, God the Son and God the Holy Spirit, and not, as has been suggested by some theologians, the heavenly host that surrounded his throne.[5] That the act of creation was the action of

---

5. See Waltke, *Old Testament Theology*, 127. As to the matter of creation, we find in the opening chapters of *Genesis* intimations of the triune existence of God. We do not concur with the argument of, for example, Bruce Waltke, who understands the "us" in Genesis 1:26 to refer to the heavenly host, not to the Persons of the Godhead. See Waltke, op. cit., 201. Nor do we concur with the firmly stated commitment to "theistic evolution" that Waltke makes as to the origin of man in ibid., 202–203. The contrary statement of John Murray in his comment on Genesis 1:26 is salutary: "To suppose that a process of evolution by forces resident in an order of things incalculably lower in the scale of being could account for man's origin, involves an incongruity once we appreciate the identity of likeness to God. Genesis 2:7 cannot be reconciled with the evolutionary hypothesis, and it confirms the conclusions derived from Genesis 1:26; 5:1; 9:6." Murray, *Collected Writings*, vol. 2, 12. Notwithstanding his attempt at explanation, Waltke's evolutionism is not rescued by the insertion of the word "theistic" before "evolution."

the Trinity of the Godhead is clarified by the facts that, first, "the *Spirit* of God moved upon the face of the waters" (Gen 1:2); and second, that it was by the *Son* that "all things were made" (John 1:3) and "by him all things [were] created, that are in heaven, and that are in earth, visible and invisible . . . all things were created by him, and for him" (Col 1:16).

Our first parent, in coming to self-consciousness, knew that he was the creature of a Creator God. Two implications follow. First, by reason that our first parent was created in "knowledge, righteousness, and holiness" (Eph 4:24; Col 3:10), two things characterized his initial state. In the first place, for Adam, to *be* was to *know*. That is to say, his very being, his consciousness and self-awareness, carried with it the knowledge and awareness of God. He did not discover God by any process of investigation or inquiry. His knowledge of God was not the result of any inductive-evidential process. It did not exist at the end of a logical syllogism. Adam knew God in a respect that was immediate and intrinsic to the very constitution of mind and soul in which he had been established. That knowledge was a derivative knowledge in that Adam, both as to his being and his knowledge, was the analogue of God. He was, that is to say, like God in every respect in which a created and finite person can be like a personal and infinite God. For that reason, Adam's knowledge, while in his finitude it was not and could not be comprehensive, was true and truly consistent with what it was that God designed for him to know. It was of course the case that further communication of God would expand Adam's knowledge and understanding. That communication was expansive when God walked with Adam "in the garden in the cool of the day" (Gen 3:8). Moreover, in man's initial state there existed a natural harmony between the faculties of soul, the mind or the intellectual faculty by which he knew God and was conscious of the mandated requirements of God, the affective faculty by which he naturally loved and reached out for communion with God, and the will or volitional faculty by which he naturally desired to please God. It is of the essence of the sin that followed that the pristine harmony of the faculties was shattered, and the hegemony of the mind was displaced by the ascendency in fallen man of the passions and the emotions.

In the second place, the condition of holiness in which Adam was created was again intrinsic to his initial state. His holiness, that is, was not a *donum superadditum*, a gift-added-on, that was in some sense granted to him following his creation. God did not at first create Adam and then communicate to him the gift of holiness.[6] Adam was, at the beginning, intrinsically and constitutionally holy. We shall see in what follows that the entrance of sin involved the loss of that initial state of holiness. Taking together the darkness of mind that ensued at the loss of the natural knowledge of God and the loss of holy state in which he first existed, Adam's fall involved a twofold disability: first, a deprivation of original character-endowments, of knowledge and holiness; and second, a depravation of soul in that the capacities and abilities of soulish faculties were disabled from their pristine competence.

The second implication of Adam's created state was that he was established as the vicegerent of God, in that he was created to be, under God, a prophet, priest, and king. In the discharge of the prophetic office he was to investigate and explain the meaning of the reality-environment in which he had come to awareness and self-consciousness. He was to be a priest in that he was privileged to have and enjoy direct communion with God who, in the preincarnate appearance of the second Person of the Godhead, walked with him "in the garden in the cool of the day." And in the priestly office Adam was to dedicate back to the glory of God his discoveries of meaning within created reality. Our first parent, in the context of those realizations, was to discharge his kingly office by ruling over all things to the glory of God. By the creation mandate, Adam was instructed: "Be fruitful, and multiply, and replenish the earth, and subdue it: and have dominion" (Gen 1:28).

The scriptural data make clear that all of God's relations with man are covenantal relations. Our first parent, that is, was established as a covenant person. What has been referred to as the covenant of works, or alternatively the covenant of creation, between God and Adam required that all of the actions of man and all of his development and progress in the world should be such as conduced to the glory of God. That is clear from the nature of Adam's prophetic, priestly, and kingly offices. Indeed, it was with the terms of that covenantal relation in view that God established Adam in a condition of probation. "And the LORD God commanded the man, saying, Of every tree of the garden thou mayest freely eat: But of the tree of the knowledge of good and evil, thou shalt not eat of it: for in the day that thou eatest thereof thou shalt surely die" (Gen 2:16–17). The fact that Adam did not continue in his initial state of

---

6. The contrary is maintained by some theologies, notably that of Roman Catholicism.

righteousness and obedience to the law of God, that he failed to sustain the terms of his probation, and the results that followed, are all too well known. In short, with Adam's dereliction from the covenantal terms of his probation in view, it can be said that therein lies the essential meaning of sin in its active character. For sin, in its essence and wherever it comes to expression, is a repudiation of covenantal obligations.

If Adam had satisfied the terms of his probation and continued in obedience to the law of God, he would have been confirmed in moral state and rewarded with eternal life. It is possible to say that the very promise of curse in the event of disobedience implied and carried with it the promise of life in the event of obedience. The covenant that God established with Adam involved, that is, the conditional promise of curse and malediction on the one hand and that of blessing and benediction on the other. That twofold aspect of God's statements to man is inherent in all of the covenantal structures and relations he has established. But the conditional promise of eternal life to Adam is not simply deducible by parity of reasoning in the manner just stated. For it became clear in due course that when Christ, who came as the second Adam to rescue us from our parlous condition, had faithfully completed his messianic-redemptive assignment, he was rewarded for his obedience to the terms of the Covenant of Grace in accordance with which he came. And by reason that the second Adam merited the reward for *his* obedience, the first Adam would have done likewise. For the first Adam was a type of the second.

The result of Adam's sin was that he was thereby disabled from fulfilling the obligations and discharging the responsibilities of his offices as prophet, priest, and king. The darkness that descended on the mind meant that he was now deprived of the true categories of interpretation of meaning that were implicit in his initial state. It was for that reason that it was necessary that Christ should come and demonstrate that in him "are hid all the treasures of wisdom and knowledge" (Col 2:3). On the levels of meaning, interpretation, and understanding, new life in Christ reestablishes for those in union with him true criteria of truth and validity in knowledge. By reason of the entrance of sin, the primeval love of God was destroyed in the human heart, and man, now a covenant-breaker, was a "hater of God" (Rom 1:30). Not only was it now true that "the god of this world hath blinded the mind" (2 Cor 4:4), but the terrible condition followed that "the natural man receiveth not the things of the Spirit of God: for they are foolishness unto him: neither can he know them, because they are spiritually discerned" (1 Cor 2:14). Man could no longer reign as God's vicegerent to discharge to the glory of God the creation mandate that had been given to him. Now he was the bonded and enslaved dupe of the devil. It was to rescue him from that enslavement that Christ came, to deliver his people from the "strong man armed" (Luke 11:21), the devil who had kept them in the somnolent security of false peace. Such was the sorry state to which Adam's fall brought himself and all his posterity, and such was the reason for Christ's going to the cross for their redemption. In the performance of his messianic-redemptive mission, Christ came "that he might destroy the works of the devil" (1 John 3:8), and that "through death he might destroy him that had the power of death, that is, the devil" (Heb 2:14). Therein lies, as we shall see more expansively, the meaning of the cross.

Adam was established, the scriptural data have stated, as the image of God. The meaning of that can be expanded as follows:

> Man, created soul and body, male and female, is the *image of God* in that he is *an immortal, rational, spiritual, moral,* and *speaking* person, capable of *reflective self-awareness* and *purposive action*, characterized in his created condition by *knowledge* and by *constitutive holiness and righteousness*, and endowed with the capacity for the reception of divine revelation, social relations and communication, and communion with God his Creator.[7]

From that, two things will be seen to follow. First, notwithstanding Adam's fall and the entrance of sin, all of his posterity remain responsible to God for the discharge of the obligations of the covenant of works under which our first parents had been established. It is a part of the reality of sin that no person since Adam has in himself or herself the ability to meet those obligations. It will accordingly follow that a highly significant aspect of the coming into the world of the eternal Son of God was that he would discharge for the people that God gave him to redeem the obligations they sustained under the covenant of works but which, by reason of their disability in the state of sin, they were unable to discharge for themselves. Further, the Scriptures again make clear that notwithstanding Adam's fall into sin and the imputation to all of his posterity of the guilt of his sin, man remains the image of God (Gen 9:6; Jas 3:9). For man remains under God an immortal, rational, spiritual,

---

7. For a more expansive discussion see Vickers, *Christian Confession*, chap. 3.

moral, and speaking person. On that ground he continues to be subject to covenantal obligations to God.

THE BIBLICAL DATA

We have referred to biblical data and their explanatory competence and authority. But in the contemporary social and intellectual culture, it is precisely that biblical competence and authority that are called in doubt or positively rejected. Why, it is asked, or on what grounds of reason, can argument be confidently founded on the Bible as the inerrant Word of God? Modern opinion argues that to rely on biblical data is transparently obscurantist. Have we not, some churchmen are now saying, climbed to a new plateau of understanding which sees the very possibility of theology and the nature of its foundation documents in a more mature and satisfying scientific perspective? The conclusion of Professor Hanson, for example, writing in the second half of the twentieth century, has only been consolidated in contemporary opinion: "The Bible . . . has been the subject of an intellectual revolution, and this revolution has affected all branches of theology. Only one hundred years ago, most Christians of all traditions would have been quite content to describe the Bible as inerrant, infallible, and inspired equally in every part. . . . The scholars . . . have absorbed this revolution. But the revolution has not reached the grass roots of Christianity. Between the average man in the pulpit and the average man or woman in the pew on the one hand and on the other the theologians and the scholars a great gulf is still fixed."[8] The discussion of the inspiration and authority of the Bible has been extensive in the evangelical church in recent years, and it cannot be maintained with confidence that the church has held consistently to the old doctrines of biblical inerrancy, infallibility, and authority.[9] The

---

8. Hanson, *Introduction* in Davidson and Leaney, *Biblical Criticism*, 9, 14.

9. The literature, which is far too extensive to be rehearsed at this point, includes at a minimum Rogers and McKim, *Authority and Interpretation of the Bible*, which was reviewed by Woodbridge, Barker, Godfrey, and Wells as cited in the bibliography. See also Gaffin, *God's Word in Servant Form* which cites the foregoing references; Enns, *Inspiration and Incarnation*, and a very valuable critical rejoinder to Enns by Scott, "The Inspiration and Interpretation of God's Word, with special reference to Peter Enns," Parts I and II. In addition to discussion of the doctrine of Scripture in Turretin, *Institutes*, vol. 1, 55–167; Bavinck, *Reformed Dogmatics*, vol. 1, 283–494; Berkhof, *Systematic Theology*, New Edition, Introductory Volume, 133–69; and Reymond, *New Systematic Theology*, 25–126, see Stonehouse and Woolley, *The Infallible Word*; Young,

gulf that Hanson conjectured as existing between the scholars and the pulpit seems clearly to have narrowed in the ensuing quarter of a century. The errant claims that the Bible is now outworn and has lost its determinative significance, and, with that, newer fashions in belief and theology, have found their way from the seminaries and the universities to the pulpit, to the loss of the common man's understanding of what the Christian gospel is and means. But to the contrary, we concur with Professor Young's counter argument that "if the Bible is not infallible, then we can be sure of nothing," and that "the fortunes of Christianity stand or fall with an infallible Bible. Attempts to evade this conclusion can only lead to self-deception."[10]

Our commitment to Scripture can be stated briefly at this introductory stage. The doctrine of Scripture embedded in the Reformed theology was crystallized in the seventeenth-century confessions: "The Old Testament in Hebrew . . . and the New Testament in Greek . . . *being immediately inspired by God*, and by his *singular care and providence* kept pure in all ages, are therefore authentical; so as in all controversies of religion, the Church is finally to appeal unto them."[11] And "the whole counsel of God, concerning all things necessary for his own glory, man's salvation, faith, and life, is either expressly set down in scripture, or by good and necessary consequences may be deduced from scripture: unto which nothing at any time is to be added, whether by new revelations of the Spirit, or traditions of men."[12]

Certain propositions follow. The Bible as we have it is, in its original autographs, the Word of God. The Bible does not *contain* the Word of God. It *is* the Word of God. By inspiration, the ultimate author of the Scriptures, the Holy Spirit, has determined that the very words of Scripture, in all their singularity and plurality, are the words of God. We hold, therefore, to the plenary, verbal, inspiration of the Scriptures. By virtue of their divine authorship the Scriptures are completely inerrant and authoritative and are the infallible rule of life and belief. As to their

---

Thy Word is Truth; Murray, *Calvin on Scripture*; Lindsell, *The Battle for the Bible*; Packer, *Beyond the Battle for the Bible*.

10. Young, *Thy Word is Truth*, 5.

11. Westminster Confession of Faith, I:8, italics added. See also The Savoy Declaration of Faith, I:8, and The Second London (Baptist) Confession, I:8.

12. Westminster Confession of Faith, I:6; likewise The Savoy Declaration and The Second London (Baptist) Confession.

authority, the Scriptures are self-attesting, and as is true of all doctrines of Christian belief we hold to the scriptural doctrine of Scripture. "All scripture is given by inspiration of God" (2 Tim 3:16). "Holy men of God spake as they were moved by the Holy Ghost" (2 Pet 1:21). And the pages of holy writ are redolent with the claim that "thus saith the Lord." The providential preservation of the Scriptures means that in proper translation we have at this time the Word of God. The canon of Scripture has been closed. Revelation has come to an end, and God has said his last word to man. God has nothing to say to man that he has not already said. But the Word of God is to be mined for the full understanding of its doctrinal content and directives, and progressive illumination thereby accrues to the Christian in his faithful submission to it.[13]

THE BEING AND HOLINESS OF GOD

Two further preliminary issues remain to provide the context in which the meaning and message of the cross are to be considered: first, a slightly expanded statement of the meaning of sin that made redemption necessary; and second, the holiness of God that the sin of our first parent, and consequently the sin of all those "descending from him by ordinary generation,"[14] has offended and outraged. I take the second of those questions first. Discussion of each will be expanded in what follows.[15]

When it is said that "God created man" (Gen 1:27) and that man as to his being and his knowledge is the derivative analogue of God, he stands, in ways we have seen, at the apex of the created reality that God spoke into existence. The worlds were created by the word of God (John 1:1–3). It follows that all of reality external to the Godhead, including persons in the image of God, are the property of God. "In him we live, and move, and have our being" (Acts 17:28). Because that is so, God is at liberty to dispose of his property as he wills. It is against that conception that the immanent and providential interventions of God in the life of the world are to be recognized. There is no more ultimate explanatory category than the will of God and what God has revealed to us as the

---

13. See the fuller discussion in chapter 7 below of the inspiration and authority of Scripture.

14. Westminster Shorter Catechism, Question 16.

15. Further discussions of issues raised in the summary paragraphs that follow are contained in Vickers, *The Fracture of Faith*, chaps. 3, 4, and 5; *When God Converts a Sinner*, chap. 3; and *The Immediacy of God*, chaps. 2 and 3.

designs and the purposed objectives of his will. But the will of God, it is also revealed, is informed by his love: first, his love for his creatures as such, to whom he conveys the benefits of his common grace; and second, his redemptive love for those whom, before the foundation of the world, he gave to his Son to redeem. "Thine they were," Christ prayed to the Father, "and thou gavest them me" (John 17:6). "Herein is love," John declared, "not that we loved God, but that he loved us, and sent his Son to be the propitiation for our sins" (1 John 4:10). We shall see, moreover, that the common or non-redemptive grace by which God conveys benefits to the world in general proceeds from, and it is significant because of, the overriding benefits that accrue from the death of Christ in establishing the right of redemption.

But lying behind God's stated purposes in love is the ineffable holiness of God himself. By his holiness we mean his separation from all that exists external to the Godhead. We speak properly of God's aseity, meaning that he is himself the cause of his own being (*a se*; from himself). He is not dependent for his own being and existence on any cause or entity or law external to himself. His knowledge of himself is immediate, in the sense that he did not discover any element or construct within his consciousness by a process of reflection or search. God knew himself and knew all things external to himself in one eternal act of knowing. He is himself Spirit, "infinite, eternal, and unchangeable in his being, wisdom, power, holiness, justice, goodness, and truth."[16] God exists in timeless eternity and has created time as a mode of finite existence. His knowledge of what eventuates in the history of the world is itself timeless, in that he has foreordained whatsoever comes to pass. God, therefore, does not wait to discover. He neither remembers nor forgets, for he knew all things in one eternal act of knowing.

The apostle John brings the realization of the holiness of God into conjunction with the meaning of redemption. First, he states at the beginning of his first epistle that "God is light, and in him is no darkness at all" (1 John 1:5). What that is saying is that God is a holy God. Second, he sets forth the possibility of fellowship with God as the end and objective of the redemption that God has provided. "If we walk in the light, as he is in the light, we have fellowship one with another [fellowship between God and the Christian believer]" (1 John 1:7). "Truly," John says, "our fellowship is with the Father, and with his Son Jesus Christ" (1

---

16. Westminster Shorter Catechism, Question 4.

John 1:3). God is a holy God. He calls on his redeemed people to be holy before him, to have nothing to do with sin that tarnishes the relation of fellowship with him (1 Pet 1:16; Lev 11:44). And while it is true, as John says in the same context, that "if we say we have no sin, we deceive ourselves," (1 John 1:8), God has made all provision for us in that "if we confess our sins, he is faithful and just to forgive us our sins, and to cleanse us from all unrighteousness" (1 John 1:9), because "the blood of Jesus Christ his Son cleanseth us from all sin" (1 John 1:7). The holiness of God, implying as it does his wrath against sin, means that "God is a consuming fire" (Heb 12:29).

The Scriptures clearly reveal that God exists as a trinity of Persons. We shall have occasion in a later chapter to consider the autotheotic nature of the Second and Third Persons of the Godhead, God the Son and God the Holy Spirit, or the fact that they are of themselves fully God. The mystery that will engage our contemplation for all eternity is that God who created time entered into time in the Person of his Son. The mystery of the incarnation of Christ is expanded to contemplate the union within his Person of the divine and the human natures. It will be necessary in that context to emphasize that Jesus Christ, when he was in this world, was not a human person. He was a divine Person who took into union with his divine nature a human nature, such that, as it was stated in what became known as the Christological settlement at the Council of Chalcedon in the year 451AD, the union of natures was "without confusion, without change, without division, and without separation." The first two of those defining characteristics explain that there was no communication of properties between the two natures, or, as Van Til puts it, "there was no commingling of the eternal and the temporal."[17] The final two defining characteristics establish the reality of the union.

Given that the eternal Son of God came into the world in the manner described, the human nature he assumed was itself a created, finite, temporal nature. Now in the heavenly places he continues to exist in that same finite, temporal human nature. It is Jesus Christ in his full personhood, in his human and his divine natures, who discharges his heavenly high priestly office. In the glorified state in which our Lord now sits in heaven, in the intercession for us and in the sympathy with which he cares for us, his human nature that was tempted in all points like as we

---

17. See Van Til, *Defense of the Faith*, 16–17.

are informs his divine personhood. He knows our frame, because he too is human. We can therefore "come boldly unto the throne of grace, that we may obtain mercy, and find grace to help in time of need" (Heb 4:16).

Jesus Christ, we say, was not a human person. He was not a divine-human person, in the sense that the divine and the human natures were combined in him in such a way that it was not possible to say that he was either uniquely divine or uniquely human. Jesus Christ was, he remained, and he is a divine person. When he came into the world he did not lay aside his glory. He remained eternally God, though he did lay aside the insignia or the signs of his glory.[18] Berkhof has grasped the significance of that in his conclusion that "the Logos assumed a human nature *that was not personalized*, that did not exist by itself."[19] Further, we hold to the mystery of the Person of Christ in that when he was in this world he was, as to his divine nature, both in the world and in heaven, as stated in the gospel reference to "the Son of man *which is in heaven*" (John 3:13, italics added), while as to his human nature he was in the world. It follows by the same token that now, as our Lord has taken his place of victory and authority at the right hand of the Father, he is, as to his human nature, in heaven, while as to his divine nature he is both in this world and in heaven.[20]

By adducing the biblical statement that Christ was a divine Person we stand aside from what have become some unfortunate claims in that respect in contemporary evangelical opinion. A tendency has emerged among theologically conservative scholars to refer to our Lord as a "human being." John Blanchard, for example, has argued that "although Jesus stands out from all the rest of humankind, he is not detached from them. He is a genuine human being."[21] Robert Peterson has presented a very valuable discussion of the fact that "*God* Became a Man for Our Salvation" in his *Calvin's Doctrine of the Atonement*.[22] In the second edition of his book, however, published under the title, *Calvin and the*

---

18. Though his miracles did attest his deity and eternal Sonship of God.

19. Berkhof, *Systematic Theology*, 321–22, italics added. See also Shedd, *Dogmatic Theology*, vol. 2, 315–29.

20. A valuable discussion of the doctrine is contained in Hendriksen, *John*, vol. 2, 500–501.

21. Blanchard, *Does God believe in atheists?* 558.

22. Peterson, *Calvin's Doctrine of the Atonement*, 11.

Atonement, Peterson has amended all such references to Christ as a "Man" to refer to him as a "Human Being."[23] In more indirect terms, Jerry Bridges and Bob Bevington have advanced the misleading doctrine by stating that "Jesus is the only human being who was truly righteous in every way."[24] The mystery of the incarnation is that the second Person of the Godhead became man, taking to himself all the faculties and capacities of human soul. He was truly man. But the integrity of doctrine must be insisted upon. It is a mistake of high importance to place our Lord, *as to the matter of his being*, on the same level as the rational beings he had created in his image. Again, Jesus Christ was not a human being; he was a divine being. When he died in his human nature he said to the Father, "into thy hands I commend my [human] spirit" (Luke 23:46). We suggest, therefore, that the requirements of christological doctrine and of doctrinal terminology point away from the designation of our Lord as a "human person" or a "human being," and make it necessary to preserve the designation of him as a divine Person (divine being).[25] Turretin, a late-seventeenth-century Reformed theologian, comments on this nexus of doctrines in an extended discussion of "The Person and State of Christ"[26] and refers to "the union of the two natures in the one person in the incarnation"[27] by stating that "the human nature . . . was destitute of proper personality and was without subsistence because otherwise it would have been a person."[28]

The eternal deity and the autotheotic nature of Christ as the Son of God are attested by his own statement that "I and my Father are one" (John 10:30). It is of interest that the "one" in that statement is in the neuter gender in the Greek text, indicating that oneness of substance is in view. The full properties of the Godhead reside in God the Son, as also in the Person of God the Holy Spirit. It is not the case that the essence of the Godhead is in some sense distributed or divided among the triune

---

23. Peterson, *Calvin and the Atonement*, 25.
24. Bridges and Bevington, *Bookends*, 24.
25. See the judicious discussion of these issues in Van Til, *Defense of the Faith*, 16.
26. Turretin, *Institutes*, vol. 2, 271–373.
27. Ibid., 310. As to the incarnation to which Turretin has referred, we shall observe in a later chapter that the union of the two natures in Christ occurred at the point of fertilization in the womb of the virgin Mary.
28. Ibid., 311. Compare the statement of Berkhof noted earlier that in Christ the human nature "was not personalized."

Persons, the Father, the Son, and the Holy Spirit. If that had been the case we should not be Trinitarians but Quaternitarians. For there would then be four entities involved: the three Persons of the Godhead, and fourthly, the essence they shared between them. But it is to be said that the full essence of the Godhead resides in each of the Persons. The divine personhood of the Holy Spirit is similarly attested by the words of Christ himself. "When he, the Spirit of truth, is come, he will guide you into all truth.... He shall glorify me: for he shall receive of mine, and shall show it unto you" (John 16:13–14). We note the personal pronouns, "he," in our Lord's reference to the Holy Spirit.

When we say that Jesus Christ was, and is, a divine Person who took a human nature, yet without sin, into union with his divine nature, we are saying also the following. Jesus Christ as he was in this world was not monophysite, or, that is, that he possessed only one nature, either human or divine. But equally, it is not to be said that he was monothelite, or that he possessed only one will. Our conclusion, on the grounds of adequate biblical data, is that there were in Christ two minds, a divine and a human, and two wills, a divine and a human. The locus of personhood was, as we have seen, the divine nature. (We shall return to the important question of the identity of our Lord). But the mystery of his incarnation is expanded and projected to the mystery of his death. For at the same time as we hold that our Lord died for his people *in his human nature*, we hold clearly that it is the *Person* of Christ to whom we look as our redeemer. It is Christ who by his perfect life and his substitutionary death has saved us. "In due time Christ died for the ungodly" (Rom 5:6).

We have said that man was created in "holiness and righteousness" and that our first parent was established as the image of God. It is not adequate to say that as a result man *bears* the image of God. We have not said that God at first created man and then impressed his image on him. We say, rather, that man *is* the image of God. Now because man as the image of God was created in holiness and righteousness, we contemplate also the holiness and righteousness of God whose image man is. Expanding briefly on what has been said of the holiness of God, consider his righteousness.

Righteousness has to do, in its essence, with conformity in action and behavior to the criteria of law. As to man's condition and status, it can be said that one is righteous, or in alternative terminology that he is "just," in so far as his relation to the law of God is what it ought to be.

The meaning of sin, in another perspective, is that it is lawlessness, or that the action of the sinner is not what it ought to be in relation to the law of God that has been promulgated to him. As to the righteousness of God, we say again that his righteousness relates to law, at this point, of course, the law of his own being. It would be the most serious of errors to imagine that there existed any law external to God's being to which he was in any respect subject, or that stood for him as criteria of action. The righteousness of God, then, exists in that in all of his deliberations, decrees, ordinations, actions, and interventions in the universe of reality he spoke into existence, he is consistent with his own holy nature. The integrity of the divine nature is expressed in the conformity to it, and the conformity to the law of his own excellence, of the affections and the will of God.

But some confusion of thought on this important point has lately entered the theology of the church. We can say, in the light of the foregoing, that because God's righteousness is exhibited in the consistency of his actions with the law of his own holy being and character, he is faithful in executing all of the demands of the covenantal promises he has made to his people. That is beyond doubt. We can therefore speak of the covenantal faithfulness of God. But it must also be said that the meaning of the biblical category of "the righteousness of God" is not exhausted by that statement. In the recent theology of the so-called New Perspective on Paul it is generally stated that the righteousness of God has reference exclusively to that single meaning. N.T. Wright, for example, one of the most prominent authors in the New Perspective tradition, has summed up the viewpoint by saying that "for a reader of . . . the Septuagint . . . 'the righteousness of God' would have one obvious meaning: God's own faithfulness to his promises, to the covenant. . . . God's righteousness is thus cognate with his trustworthiness."[29]

But more, and something radically different, is involved. The apostolic explanation of the redemption that Christ accomplished states that "He [God] made Him [Christ] who knew no sin to be sin for us, that we might become the *righteousness of God* in Him" (2 Cor 5:21 [NKJV], italics added). What is to be said, then, of "the righteousness of God" in that clearly redemptive context? What is involved is that though the sinner stands before God in a state of unrighteousness, God imputes to him, or places to his account, the righteousness of Christ. A remarkable

---

29. Wright, *What Saint Paul Really Said*, 96.

transference has taken place. A double imputation has occurred. The guilt of the repentant sinner's sin has been imputed to Christ, and the righteousness of Christ, the merit of his perfect active obedience in fulfilling all of the demands of the law of God and his passive obedience in dying on the sinner's behalf in obedience to the law, has been imputed to the sinner. God is righteous in transferring the righteousness of Christ to the people for whom Christ died, and those beneficiaries of the death of Christ are then regarded as themselves righteous in the sight of God.

But the New Perspective on Paul theology will have nothing to do with the fact or the doctrine of imputation. Wright sums up the case in the following terms. Consider God in Christ as the judge with whom we have to do. "If we use the language of the law court, it makes no sense whatever to say that the judge imputes, imparts, bequeaths, conveys or otherwise transfers his righteousness to either the plaintiff or the defendant. Righteousness is not an object, a substance or a gas which can be passed across the courtroom. . . . To imagine the defendant somehow receiving the judge's righteousness is simply a category mistake. That is not the way language works."[30] The righteousness of God was not something that could be transferred to another person by imputation. In that critical failure to grasp the essence of biblical doctrine as it bears on the reality of redemption lies the bankruptcy of much of contemporary theological opinion.

SIN

Sin, as to its essence, we have said, is the repudiation of covenantal obligations. In that statement we contemplate the fact that because man is the image of God, because he is by creation the property of God, he lives under an inescapable obligation to the law of God. For that reason the apostle John could say that "sin is the transgression of the law" (1 John 3:4). The Westminster Shorter Catechism puts the matter in comprehensive and covenantal terms. Adducing the terms of the first covenant that God made with Adam, it concludes that "the covenant being made with Adam, not only for himself, but for his posterity, all mankind, descending from him by ordinary generation [excluding thereby the human birth of Christ], sinned in him, and fell with him in his first

---

30. Ibid., 98.

transgression."[31] The question before us now is not that of why God, in his creative decree, should have established Adam as the federal head or the representative head of the race. The reality is that according to his wisdom and the dictates of his will God has constituted all mankind in that relationship. We have no prerogative to question beyond that point of reality. The state of sin in which all mankind finds itself, therefore, is directly traceable to, and is directly the result of its participation in, Adam's fall. But having taken note that the fall "brought mankind into the estate of sin and misery," the Catechism proceeds: "The sinfulness of that estate whereinto man fell, consists in the guilt of Adam's first sin, the want of original righteousness, and the corruption of his whole nature, which is commonly called *original sin*, together with all actual transgressions which proceed from it."[32]

The letter to the Romans states the case in precise terms. "As by one man sin entered into the world, and death by sin; and so death passed upon all men, for that all have sinned" (Rom 5:12); "by one man's offence death reigned by one" (Rom 5:17); "by the offence of one judgment came upon all men to condemnation" (Rom 5:18); and "by one man's disobedience many were made sinners" (Rom 5:19). The reality is that by virtue of our solidarity with Adam, when Adam sinned, we sinned. "In Adam all die" (1 Cor 15:22).

It follows, as to the meaning of sin, that sin is not in the first place a matter of action or behavior. Sin has to do, first, with the state into which we were reduced by Adam's fall. That is why the Catechism begins its explanation by stating that the fall brought mankind into the *estate* of sin and misery.[33] It is for that reason that emphasis must be given to the disabilities of soulish faculties, consequent on the imputation to us of the guilt of Adam's sin, that do themselves give rise to actions of sin. The first thing to be understood is what the Catechism has referred to as "original sin." Sinful actions follow from the state and condition of sin to which we were reduced. It is all an instance of the fact that being is prior to doing. In other words, it is not true that we are sinners because we commit sin. The contrary is true. We commit sin because we are sinners; that is, because we were constituted sinners at Adam's fall, and we therefore come into the world in a state of sin. The translation of the Greek

---

31. Westminster Shorter Catechism, Question 16.
32. Ibid., Questions 17–18, italics added.
33. Ibid., Question 17.

text at Romans 5:19 requires it to be noted that "by one man's [Adam's] disobedience many were *constituted* sinners."

But the meaning of sin is not understandable until we first confront the holiness of God. For sin, whether it is conceived of as state or action, is whatever outrages and offends the holiness of God, his transcendent majesty-holiness, his supreme perfections and his essential glory as reflected in the law he has given for our mandate and guidance. His glory is exhibited throughout the Scriptures. The song of Moses moves to its climax with the confession: "Who is like unto thee, O LORD . . . who is like thee, glorious in holiness?" (Exod 15:11). The strain is taken up in the song of Hannah following the birth of Samuel: "My heart rejoiceth in the LORD . . . There is none holy as the LORD: for there is none beside thee" (1 Sam 2:1–2). The prophet Isaiah knew that he bore the words of "the high and lofty One that inhabiteth eternity, whose name is Holy" (Isa 57:15), and Isaiah reports his vision of God's glory: "I saw also the Lord sitting upon a throne, high and lifted up, and . . . the seraphim [who] cried . . . Holy, holy, holy, is the LORD of hosts; the whole earth is full of his glory" (Isa 6:1–3). The prophet's reaction to the majesty-holiness of God called forth his "woe is me! for I am undone; because I am a man of unclean lips, and I dwell in the midst of a people of unclean lips; for mine eyes have seen the King, the LORD of hosts " (Isa 6:5). The scriptural data could be multiplied.

God's holiness implies his revulsion from sin, his abhorrence of sin, and the incompatibility of sin and uncleanness with his holy character. The prophet Habakkuk has observed: "O LORD my God, mine Holy One. . . . Thou art of purer eyes than to behold evil, and canst not look on iniquity" (Hab 1:12–13). We must speak, then, of God's vehement hatred of sin. He hates what he sees as the very beginnings of sin in the hearts and imaginations of his creatures. The prophet Zechariah has observed: "Let none of you imagine evil in your hearts . . . for all these are things that I hate, saith the LORD" (Zech 8:17). In his holy revulsion from evil God uses the strongest of language, "I hate, I despise" (Amos 5:21), and regarding his people because of their sin he says: "My soul hateth: they are a trouble unto me; I am weary to bear them" (Isa 1:14). Of the sin of idolatry that was an offence to him, God says: "Oh, do not this abominable thing that I hate" (Jer 44:4). The sin of his people "vexed his holy Spirit" (Isa 63:10). God makes it abundantly clear that his detestation of sin involves hatred that is directed against not only the sin, but the person of the sinner. "Because thou hast not remembered the days of thy youth, but hast fretted me in all these things; behold, therefore I also will recompense thy way upon thine head, saith the Lord GOD: and thou shalt not commit this lewdness above all thine abominations" (Ezek 16:43). The Psalmist underlines the gravity of sin in his address to God: "Thou hatest all workers of iniquity" (Ps 5:5).

Stephen Charnock, the seventeenth-century Puritan, concludes in his very valuable work on *The Existence and Attributes of God* that "God being the highest, most absolute and infinite holiness, doth infinitely, and therefore intensely, hate unholiness; being infinitely righteous, doth infinitely abhor unrighteousness; being infinitely true, doth infinitely abhor falsity, as it is the greatest and most deformed evil. As it is from the righteousness of his nature that he hath a content and satisfaction in righteousness, 'The righteous Lord loveth righteousness' (Ps 11:7), so it is from the same righteousness of his nature that he detests whatever is morally evil. As his nature therefore is infinite, so must his abhorrence be."[34]

It is necessary to avoid at this point confusion between finitude and sin. It is not true to say that evil inheres in man simply by virtue of a privation that exists because of the limitations of his creaturehood. Man as he came from the hands of his Creator was constitutionally, intrinsically holy. He was created in a state of *posse non peccare*, possible not to sin, but in his finitude he was mutable, defectible, and in the exercise of his will he fell from "the estate wherein [he was] created."[35] The occasion of Adam's fall was that he made his false and damning assertion of autonomy against God. He would not, he said, remain subject to the criteria of action and true belief that God had communicated to him. He would henceforth be a law unto himself. He would find, as he claimed, adequate criteria of wisdom, belief, and action within himself or within the world that surrounded him.

But sin carries with it further implications. Sin, or moral evil, consists in the opposite of the love of God. It is opposition to God. It is separation from God. Berkhof has summed it up by commenting that sin is "separation from God, opposition to God, hatred of God [that] manifests itself in constant transgression of the law of God in thought, word, and deed."[36] The law of God, encapsulated in its moral aspect in

---

34. Charnock, *Existence and Attributes of God*, 456.
35. Compare Westminster Shorter Catechism, Question 13.
36. Berkhof, *Systematic Theology*, 232.

the Ten Commandments, is summarized in the directive that "thou shalt love the Lord thy God with all thy heart, and with all thy soul, and with all thy mind" (Matt 22:37). If we have done that we have kept the law. If we have not done that, the condemnation of God rests upon us, and in that case our only rescue and relief, the ground of our hope for reconciliation and peace with God, is the substitutionary work and obedience of Christ. The cross of Christ is again the refuge for sinners.

Our first parent's sin, while it led to the state of separation from God, was itself an ethical lapse. It was ethical in the sense that Adam did what he should not have done. He ate the forbidden fruit. When we say that sin was ethical and not metaphysical, we are saying that the entrance of sin did not effect any change in man's essential being as, in creaturely finitude, he stood before God and under obligation to God. Sin, in other words, did not represent a fall to a lower level in some imagined chain of being. But the ethical lapse that constituted our first parent's sin did have implications for the soul, in that it brought upon it the spiritual death that God had promised would be the result of sin. Now the faculties of the soul were depraved. The mind was darkened (2 Cor 4:4), man was now a God-hater (Rom 1:30), naturally the enemy of God (Rom 8:7), and the slave of Satan and sin (Luke 11:21; John 8:44). Christ responded to the Jews on one dramatic occasion: "Why do ye not understand my speech? even because ye cannot hear my word. Ye are of your father the devil, and the lusts of your father ye will do" (John 8:43–44).

By his fall into sin man not only forfeited and lost his communion with God, but he became, by that fatal act, enslaved to sin. When, on a memorable occasion, the Jews insisted to Christ that they were "never in bondage to any man," Christ replied that "whosoever committeth sin is the servant of sin" (John 8:33–34), or the slave of sin, or in bondage to sin. The apostle Peter made the same point in his argument that "of whom a man is overcome, of the same he is brought in bondage" (2 Pet 2:19). Paul had explained to the Romans that "to whom ye yield yourselves servants to obey, his servants [slaves] ye are . . . whether of sin unto death, or of obedience unto righteousness" (Rom 6:16). At the fall, that is, man lost his free will. Given the depravation of the faculties of soul, man from that point on is either the slave of Satan or, by the renewing, recreating work of the Spirit of God in the soul, the willing slave of Christ.

Questions no doubt swirl in the context we have raised. Is man not in any sense free? Is he not a free, responsible agent? Yes, we hold under the Scriptures to man's free agency and responsibility. But within the orbit of sin, and of the possibility of redemption from sin and of eternal salvation, we are not talking of free agency. We are talking of what we have referred to as free will. Man has free agency in the sense that he is free to be consistent with his own nature. In that sense all creatures are free to be consistent with their natures. A horse is free to be a horse, a cow a cow. Or, in the expressive language of the apostle Peter, a sow is free to be a sow, but only a sow. One can take a sow and wash it, Peter observes. But all one will have will be a washed sow. It will always be a sow, nothing other than a sow. And the only expectation we can have of it is, as Peter says, that it will return to its "wallowing in the mire" (2 Pet 2:22).

In the same sense, man has free agency. Man in sin, man in his unregenerate nature, is free only to be consistent with that nature. And that nature, the Scriptures attest, is a sinful nature. Man in sin is free, then, only to be sinful. It is his nature to be sinful. It is only then by the intervening, redeeming, renewing, recreating grace of God set forth by virtue of the death of Christ on the cross that any sinner can be saved.

We observe finally in relation to sin that Adam's fall involved for all of his posterity a twofold effect that is implied in what has already been said: first, the immediate imputation to all that came from him by ordinary generation of the guilt of his first sin; and second, the transmission to them of a fallen nature.[37] We shall see in what follows the meaning of the work of the Spirit of God in the creation within the soul of a new and godly nature. But until that sovereign work of God is done, by reason of the application to the sinner of the benefits of what Christ accomplished for sinners in his death on the cross, sin in any of its expressions is, for the sinner, self-directed. By that we mean that as sin takes hold of a man, the passions and energies of his soul are directed not towards his Creator to whom he is obligated, but towards himself. Man in sin has made for himself a god in his own image. He is effectively a god unto himself.

But there is a gospel remedy. It is grounded in the love of God that established his Covenant of Grace that set forth a redemption for his people. In sending his Son into the world he has set forth a propitiation for sin, against the demands of his holy justice and law. In Christ, the

---

37. For a fuller discussion of the immediate imputation of Adam's sin see Vickers, *The Immediacy of God*, chap. 3.

repentant, believing sinner is a new creation. In the chapters that follow we shall address more fully the meaning of the redemption that Christ accomplished by his death on the cross and the respects in which the benefits are transmitted to those whom he came to redeem.

2

Biblical Foundations

THE CROSS OF CHRIST was not an accident of history. The fact that the death of Christ on the cross was ordained in the council of the Godhead before the foundation of the world opens to our view the covenantal decrees of God, the implementation of which led to the cross. In his sermon on the Day of Pentecost the apostle Peter declared forthrightly to the Jews: "Ye men of Israel, hear these words; Jesus of Nazareth . . . *being delivered by the determinate counsel and foreknowledge of God*, ye have taken, and by wicked hands [that is, with the collaboration in Christ's death of the Roman authorities] have crucified and slain" (Acts 2:22–23, italics added). The events of that darkened day were no accident of history. Again, when the disciples were shortly thereafter gathered together in prayer, they recognized and acknowledged to God that what "Herod, and Pontius Pilate, with the Gentiles, and the people of Israel" had done in the death of Jesus was "whatsoever thy hand and thy counsel determined before to be done" (Acts 4:27–28). Here we are brought face to face with God's covenantal arrangements and promises in the life of his people, in the coming into the world and the death of his Son on their behalf and their ultimate salvation by the redemption that Christ provided.

THE COVENANTAL DECREES AND THE BEING OF GOD

The key to the Scriptures, the basic hermeneutical principle or the principle of interpretation in terms of which we hear the scriptures speak, is located in the covenant of salvation by which God has ordered his redemptive relations with his people. We have already referred to the Covenant of Works, or the Covenant of Creation, the repudiation of whose obligations constituted Adam's fall into sin. But in the context of the entailment of sin and the unfolding history of the world, it was God's eternally declared purpose to save a people for himself from the race of Adam and his posterity. Behind the initial covenant that God made with our first parents, therefore, stand the eternal divine decrees. From the predeterminate council of the Godhead there proceeded, first, the Covenant of Redemption between the divine Persons, God the Father, God the Son, and God the Holy Spirit (Acts 2:22-23, 4:27-28, 15:18; Eph 1:11; 1 Pet 1:2).

It is extensively clear on the pages of Scripture that in that council the divine Persons undertook respective redemptive offices. It was the redemptive office of the Father to elect a numberless host to salvation and to give them to his Son to redeem. God "hath chosen us in [Christ] before the foundation of the world," the apostle Paul stated to the Ephesians, "having predestinated us unto the adoption of children by Jesus Christ to himself" (Eph 1:4-5; See also John 17:6, 9). It was the redemptive office of the Son to come into the world "when the fulness of the time was come" (Gal 4:4), to be born of a virgin, to take a sinless human nature into union with his divine nature, to satisfy all of the demands of the law of God on behalf of the people the Father had given him, and to bear in his death the penalty for their sin. Again, Christ died for sinners (1 Tim 1:15); he died "for the ungodly" (Rom 5:6). The redemptive office of the Holy Spirit was that he should apply to those for whom Christ died the gifts and benefits that Christ purchased for them in his death. In doing so, he would convey to them by his sovereign grace the blessing of sanctification that would conform them to the likeness of Christ, and thus he would conduct them to glory. The objectives of that decree of redemption are implicit in the reference of the apostle Peter to the "elect according to the foreknowledge of God the Father, through sanctification of the Spirit, unto obedience and sprinkling of the blood of Jesus Christ" (1 Pet 1:2).

The *parties* to the Covenant of Redemption were thus the three Persons of the Godhead, and the *subjects* of the covenant were the host that God chose and destined to be saved. Those subjects were the fallen offspring of Adam who, in the mind and the eternal vision of God were lost in sin but salvable by his grace set forth in Christ. Mystery, of course, inheres in all that we have said. It is beyond our finite competence to understand or plumb the depths of the intratrinitarian communication that we have referred to as the council of the Godhead. The very conception of the council of the Godhead raises in the mind the notion of communication in time, or a temporal communication process, whereas God exists outside of time, in timeless eternity, before the creation of time. We bow before the mystery. And we recognize, as was stated in an earlier context, that because the full essence of the Godhead resides fully in each of the divine Persons, each is in full possession of the divine mind, the divine attributes in which the essence of God comes to expression, and the divine will.

We hold to the predeterminate council of the Godhead and, on the grounds of the scriptural data, to the intracommunication between the triune divine Persons, each possessing distinguishable properties though existing in the unity and singularity of the Godhead. Of course at this point we confront the mystery of God in his being and personhood. Again we bow before it. Because the being and purpose and absolute personhood of God, of which man is the derivative analogue, stands behind all reality external to the Godhead, we find in what God has revealed concerning himself the resolution of what has puzzled the minds of thoughtful men and philosophers throughout the ages. We take brief note of that puzzle because of its relevance to what we are about to observe as the ground and unity of all meaning in God.

A problem that faces our best thought in the search for the meaning of reality is what we refer to as that of unity and plurality, of the relation of individual things to what it is that gives them coherence and unified explanation. In the history of thought it has been referred to as the problem of the one-and-the-many. Cornelius Van Til, a prominent Reformed apologist-theologian in the twentieth century, has rightly observed on it as follows: "The philosophers have sought for a unified outlook on human experience. Philosophers have sought for as comprehensive a picture of the nature of reality as a whole as man is able to attain. But the universe is composed of many things. Man's problem is to find unity in the midst of the plurality of things."[1] Van Til continues: "In seeking for an answer to the One-and-Many question . . . [the] *many* must be brought into contact with one another. But how do we know that they can be brought into contact with one another? How do we know that the many do not simply exist as unrelated particulars? . . . In such a case we should know nothing of them; they would be abstracted from the body of knowledge that we have; they would be *abstract* particulars. On the

1. Van Til, *Defense of the Faith*, 24.

other hand, how is it possible that we should obtain a unity that does not destroy the particulars? We seem to get our unity by generalizing, by abstracting from the particulars in order to include them in larger unities. If we keep up this process of generalization till we exclude all particulars . . . have we then not stripped these particulars of their particularity? Have we then obtained anything but an *abstract* universal?"[2]

Now it is necessary to observe that our doctrine of God is vitally relevant to, and that it supplies the answer to, those very questions. That is because the problem of the one-and-the-many, of unity and plurality, is resolved in what God has revealed as to his being and his ordinations. Because God has revealed himself as the eternally existing triune being, one God in three Persons, of one substance, he is the absolute universal in whom the distinguishable properties of the Father, the Son, and the Holy Spirit consist. "In God's being there are no particulars not related to the universal and there is nothing universal that is not fully expressed in the particulars."[3] The solution to the conceptual problem of unity and plurality exists in the fact that in God unity and plurality are equally ultimate and eternal. And because God has spoken all aspects of created reality into existence and has ordered all the facts and all the relations between the facts that describe that reality, the particulars of reality accord with the universal laws that God has created and established.

We may put that in different terms. What Van Til has referred to as the philosophers' problem can alternatively be stated as that of the search for the explanation of the meaning of reality. That, in short, the search for explanation, is the basic meaning-task of philosophy. It can be said, by way of digression, that the discovery and statement of explanation was the objective of the prophetic office given to Adam at the creation. The objective of prophecy is to explain what God has declared, as to being and morality, what bearing that has on the meaning and interpretation of reality, and how the rational creatures of God should therefore conduct their lives in the world. The Old Testament prophets also were concerned with precisely that, to explain the nature of God's self-disclosure of his being and attributes and to call his people to levels of morality consistent with that disclosure.

Given that the objective of human thought is essentially that of explanation, notably at this point the explanation of reality and of the

2. Ibid., 25–26.
3. Ibid., 26.

locus of unity in all things, it follows from God's revelation that it is in him that absolute being exists, absolute personality, and absolute knowledge, purpose, morality, and truth. All aspects of reality external to the Godhead are what they are, and they acquire the meaning they possess, because of their origination in the will of God and his sustaining them by his providence. There is no locus of explanation beyond the being and will of God, as that will is informed by his love for his creatures and, in a particular sense that follows from the atonement he set forth in his Son, his love for the people he has redeemed.

That absoluteness of being and knowledge in God, and its derivative implications for human understanding, are clearly stated in the Scriptures. The second Person of the Godhead came into the world to become Jesus Christ in order to "declare" the Father to us (John 1:18). He came in order to reveal God to us. "He that hath seen me hath seen the Father," he said to one of his incredulous disciples (John 14:9), because, as he had already said, "I and my Father are one" (John 10:30). For that reason, the apostle Paul could later say that "in whom [Christ] are hid all the treasures of wisdom and knowledge" (Col 2:3). Jesus Christ in himself, that is to say, is the final and absolute locus of explanation of all things, for in him alone are found the true and adequate principles of interpretation and the criteria of validity and truth in knowledge. That is confirmed, in turn, by what God has stated as the relation of Jesus Christ to the eschatological terminus to which, by divine ordination, the whole creation moves. "In the dispensation of the fulness of times," he has said, he will "gather together in one all things in Christ, both which are in heaven, and which are on the earth; even in him" (Eph 1:10).

But if the problem of the explanation of all reality is resolved in the being and the self-disclosure of God in Christ, it remains to ask what it is that orders, maintains, and directs the progressive unfolding of reality until the day that has been ordained as God's eschatological terminus. The answer again is in the Person and the disclosure of Christ. We have seen that he is the Lord of creation, that all things "that are in heaven, and that are in earth, visible and invisible . . . were created by him, and for him" (Col 1:16). But beyond that, it is by his power, purpose, and providence that "all things consist" (Col 1:17) or, as an alternative translation has it, that all things are held together (ESV). It is by Christ that all things are upheld, occupy their place in the divinely ordained scheme of history for the world, cohere in their interdependent determination of outcomes, and are conducted to their ordained conclusion. The writer of the letter to the Hebrews had the same conception in mind when he refers to the Son of God as, by divine appointment, "upholding all things [or 'the universe,' as another translation (ESV) states it] by the word of his power" (Heb 1:3). The fundamental problem of human thought is therefore resolved. All explanation finds its terminus in the self-disclosure that God has made in Christ. Absoluteness, in being and knowledge, and therefore unity of explanation in the derivative knowledge that is available to man as the finite creature of God, resides in God and his self-disclosure in Christ.

We may reflect further on our relation to the mystery of the triune being of God, as that bears on our studies of the meaning of the cross. Consider, for example, the works of God internal to the Godhead, the *opera ad intra* of God. These are in essence threefold. They have generally gone under the theological headings of generation, spiration, and divine council. "Generation" refers to the eternal generation of the Son by the Father. Berkhof has summarized that in definitional terms as follows: "It is that eternal and necessary act of the first person in the Trinity, whereby He, within the divine Being, is the ground of a second personal subsistence like His own, and puts this second person in possession of the whole divine essence, without any division, alienation, or change."[4] "Spiration" refers to the breathing forth within the Godhead of the Person of the Holy Spirit. Berkhof again summarizes that as "that eternal and necessary act of the first and second persons in the Trinity whereby they, within the divine Being, become the ground of the personal subsistence of the Holy Spirit, and put the third person in possession of the whole divine essence, without any division, alienation, or change."[5] The third aspect of the *opera ad intra* of God refers to the determination of the divine decrees that we have already referred to.

But the veil of understanding that stands between us and the infinite God has not been drawn, and cannot be drawn, to provide a comprehensive entry to the deliberations of the divine mind. Now in the same way as we bow before the mystery of the being of God and his triune, eternal existence, so we bow before the scriptural revelation of God's purposes in his covenantal establishments and, as we shall go on to see, in his sincere offer of the gospel. When the apostle acknowledged that

---

4. Berkhof, *Systematic Theology*, 94.
5. Ibid., 97.

"great is the mystery of godliness," he adduced important aspects of the orbit of mystery: "God was manifest in the flesh, justified in the Spirit, seen of angels, preached unto the Gentiles, believed on in the world, received up into glory" (1 Tim 3:16). We bear in mind continuously that there is mystery for us in our finitude, but there is no mystery for God. Because in our creaturehood we are the analogue of God both as to our knowledge and our being, we may, and we do, have *true* knowledge of God and of what has occurred in the mind of God, but we do not have *comprehensive* knowledge. We do not know as God knows. And we do not have any capacity to marshal in thought all of the relationships in all of the structures of knowledge that God has ordained and set forth. Our knowledge differs from that of God, not only quantitatively, but also and most notably, qualitatively.

While distinguishable redemptive offices were undertaken by the respective Persons of the Godhead, it remains true that in all of the works of God external to the Godhead, the *opera ad extra*, the three divine Persons are jointly engaged. It need only be said at this point, for example, that it was uniquely the Person of Christ who came and died on the cross in his human nature. It was God the Son who suffered for his people, not God the Father. In the early church some did, in fact, attempt to state that the Father did suffer, thereby giving rise to what became known as the false doctrine of Patripassianism. But that never became accepted dogma of the church. As to the joint activities of the Persons of the Godhead in redemption, we hear Christ say that "I am in the Father, and the Father in me. The words that I speak unto you I speak not of myself: but the Father that dwelleth in me, he doeth the works" (John 14:10). Further, we have it clearly stated that Christ in this world was supported in his messianic mission by the Holy Spirit. "For he whom God hath sent . . . God giveth not the Spirit by measure unto him" (John 3:34). When Christ was baptized in the Jordan, "the Spirit of God descending on him like a dove" came upon him and the Father testified that "this is my beloved Son, in whom I am well pleased" (Matt 3:16–17). And the writer to the Hebrews states that it was "through the eternal Spirit" that Christ "offered himself without spot to God" (Heb 9:14).

In that manner, we have the divine disclosure of the objectives of the Covenant of Redemption that was formed in the predeterminate divine council. But in order that those objectives should be realized in time and in fact, it was necessary that an implementing covenant should be established between God and the elect whom he had chosen to redeem. We have, therefore, the Covenant of Grace, the *parties* to which were God on the one hand and, on the other, his people as represented by Christ. In terms of that covenant, Christ actually undertook and discharged all that had been committed to him in the Covenant of Redemption. He actually died for his people, and in virtue of that death all of the benefits conceived by the grace of God as their potential property actually, and in due time, accrued to them. "For this cause he [Christ] is the mediator of the new testament, that by means of death, for the redemption of the transgressions that were under the first testament, they which are called might receive the promise of eternal inheritance [or, that is, the inheritance that had been promised]" (Heb 9:15).

The covenants of God that are thus directed to the salvation of his elect can be viewed alternatively in terms of the divine decrees to elect, to redeem, and to call and sanctify a people for God himself. In that context, we may observe the identity of the subjects of the respective decrees. The question has arisen in the history of doctrine as to who it was for whom Christ died. It has been claimed by some, notably those of Arminian persuasion, that Christ died "for all men indiscriminately" or, that is, that in his death he bore the sins of all men. Such a *general* or *universal*, as opposed to what we shall refer to as a *particular*, view of the atonement that Christ offered argues that in his death Christ, in a unique sense, made salvation possible for all men. The outcome, then, as to who would in fact be saved depended on whether particular individuals accepted or rejected the offer of salvation that had already been effected for them. In that scheme of things, it is clear that individual salvation turns ultimately on the sovereign decision of the individual person himself. Christ has done his part, it is claimed, and now if eternal life is to be gained, the individual must do his part. That, in other words, amounts to a doctrine of autosoterism, or the implication that man saves himself. It implies the sovereignty in salvation of the individual. God is thereby robbed of his sovereignty. But holding to what we have already seen as the divine Covenant of Redemption, it is clear that the biblical doctrine is not that of autosoterism in the sense just envisaged. It is a doctrine of a divine monergism. God saves his people entirely by the operation of his grace that his love for his people set forth on their behalf. "By grace are ye saved," Paul insisted to the Ephesians, and that, he said, is "the gift of God" (Eph 2:8). Christ did not die merely to make salvation possible. In his death he actually saved his people.

The system of doctrine from which we dissent states, then, that while Christ died "for all men indiscriminately," only those are saved who believe. And only to them, therefore, does the Holy Spirit apply the gifts and benefits of Christ's redemption. What that involves, it will be clear, is that the subjects of God's decree to redeem and the subjects of his decree to call and sanctify are not the same set of people. Christ died for *all* men it is said, but the Holy Spirit applies the benefits of his death to only *some* men. In that event, a wedge is driven between the subjects of the respective decrees. But if in that manner a wedge is driven between the *work* of Christ and the *work* of the Holy Spirit, a wedge is thereby driven between the *knowledge* of Christ and the *knowledge* of the Holy Spirit. But further, if, in that way, a wedge is driven between the *work* and the *knowledge* of the divine Persons, a wedge is thereby driven between the *being* of the Persons of the Godhead. In that event the doctrine of God, of the unity and singularity of the Godhead, has fallen to the ground. The fact and the doctrine to be held is that those whom God elected and gave to the Son to redeem were precisely and in their particular identities the ones for whom Christ died. They, then, are precisely the ones whom the Holy Spirit will call and sanctify and bring to glory. The subjects of the divine decrees to elect, to redeem, and to glorify were identical people, conceived in the mind and the love of God before the foundation of the world.

The Lord himself entertained precisely that awareness as to the scope and objectives of his death. When, in his extensive discourse on his mission and objectives as the good shepherd who gives his life for his sheep, he said that "I lay down my life for the sheep" (John 10:15), he clarified the definitiveness of his atonement. "I give unto them eternal life," he said, "and they shall never perish" (John 10:28). On that occasion certain of the Jews, who were still incredulous and who protested uncertainty as to his identity, came to him and asked him to clarify still further whether he was in fact the Christ who should come. "Tell us plainly," they said (John 10:24). Our Lord's response was startling in its import and depth. "Ye believe not," he said, "because ye are not of my sheep" (John 10:26).

That statement means that the atonement of Christ was a *particular* atonement. That is, he died for particular people. He died for the subjects of the Covenant of Grace. The contrary view falls under the weight of its own logic. For it must confront the question of the scope and effectiveness of the atonement for sin that the death of Christ involved. What are we to say of his death? When he died his substitutionary death, Christ bore *all* the sins of all men, or *some* of the sins of all men, or, as the doctrine of particular atonement maintains, all of the sins of some men. If he bore all of the sins of all men, then all will be saved. The justice of God could not project eternal damnation to those for whose sins his Son had already paid the penalty his law demanded. The notion of a universal atonement implies of necessity universal salvation. In that case the biblical doctrine that is spread liberally on the pages of Scripture, that of the eternal punishment of those who do not repent, is vacated. If, on the other hand, Christ bore only some of the sins of all men, then no person at all can be saved, for every individual will then remain obligated to bear the eternal punishment for the sins that the atonement of Christ has not covered. It might be said from the Arminian doctrinal perspective that while Christ did, in fact, make a general or universal atonement, nevertheless those will fail of eternal life who continue in unbelief. Their eternal perdition, then, is due to their refusal of the benefits that the atonement of Christ has freely offered them. But the argument fails by reason that unbelief is in itself a capital, we may say the ultimate, sin, and if that sin remains, it cannot be maintained that Christ did, in fact, bear the penalty of *all* sin. The residual sin of unbelief has remained outside the scope of effectiveness of the atonement. Such a claim that might be made as a potential Arminian response falls under the weight of its own inconsistency.

When we reflect on God's Covenant of Grace and his decree of election to salvation, the remarkable reality that forces itself upon us is not that God chose only some of his fallen creatures and did not choose them all. The remarkable thing is that God's mercy was such that he chose any. For all of those descending from Adam by ordinary generation stood under the curse of sin and warranted only the eternal perdition that God's original covenant had, for that reason, promised. The Westminster Confession has concluded luminously on the point: "As God hath appointed the elect unto glory, so hath he, by the eternal and most free purpose of his will, foreordained all the means thereunto."[6] But what of the rest of mankind? The Confession continues: "The rest

---

6. Westminster Confession of Faith, III:6.

of mankind, God was pleased, according to the unsearchable counsel of his own will, whereby he extendeth or withholdeth mercy as he pleaseth, for the glory of his sovereign power over his creatures, *to pass by*, and to ordain them to dishonour and wrath *for their sin*, to the praise of his glorious justice."[7]

In the history of theological debate, differences of view have ensued regarding what has been referred to as the equal ultimacy of God's decrees of election and reprobation. The italicized phrases in the statement we have just observed from the Westminster Confession bear on the issue. In the counsel and foreordination of God he did, as was said, "pass by" certain individuals. That is, he did, for reasons of his own will, refrain from electing them to salvation. The ground of that decision of choice is unattainable to us in the divine will. That divine action of "passing by" is referred to in theological terms as "preterition." Beyond that, those whom God passed by were left and condemned to the eternal perdition that their sin warranted. The Confession has judiciously noted that it was "for their sin" that their condemnation ensued. The action of God to that effect is referred to in theological terms as "reprobation."

What is at issue, then, is that the ground of God's act of *preterition* is his own will. The ground of the sinner's *reprobation* is his or her own sin. There is a true sense in which equal ultimacy attaches to all of the decrees of God, here election and reprobation. But the grounds of the outcomes consist in the dictates of God's will on the one hand and on the sinner's sin on the other. We conclude regarding God's salvific decrees that his grace he has addressed to our guilt, and his mercy he has addressed to the misery in which we would otherwise have been bound for all eternity. God in his ineffable holiness is "just, and the justifier of him which believeth in Jesus" (Rom 3:26). Well might the Psalmist exclaim: "Mercy and truth are met together; righteousness and peace have kissed each other" (Ps 85:10).

THE FREE OFFER OF THE GOSPEL

It is part of the biblical mandate that the gospel of salvation is to be offered to all men, and the free and universal offer of salvation through belief in Christ is to be preserved. That means that while the atonement Christ effected is not an indiscriminate atonement, nevertheless the

---

7. Ibid., III:7, italics added.

benefits of it are to be offered indiscriminately to all. We do not have an *indiscriminate atonement*, but we have mandated in the Scriptures an *indiscriminate offer of salvation*. There is no contradiction is what has been said.

The gospel of salvation is a gospel of "whosoever." "God so loved the world [the world of men in general], that he gave his only begotten Son, that whosoever believeth in him should not perish, but have everlasting life" (John 3:16). And that free and open invitation of the gospel is spread liberally across the pages of Scripture. At the very end of the final book of Revelation the invitation is confirmed: "Let him that is athirst come. And whosoever will, let him take of the water of life freely" (Rev 22:17). We hear the echoes of the words of the prophet: "Ho, every one that thirsteth, come ye to the waters, and he that hath no money; come ye, buy, and eat; yea, come, buy wine and milk without money and without price" (Isa 55:1). The gospel of the grace of God is freely offered. Its terms are simple and clear: "If thou shalt confess with thy mouth the Lord Jesus, and shalt believe in thine heart that God raised him from the dead, thou shalt be saved" (Rom 10:9). In straightforward terms Paul replied to the Philippian jailor, "believe on the Lord Jesus Christ, and thou shalt be saved" (Acts 16:31).

We recall that on a memorable occasion our Lord delivered his remarkable discourse on his identity as the bread of life. Not all his hearers believed on him. But he declared that "all that the Father giveth me shall come to me; and him that cometh to me I will in no wise cast out" (John 6:37). In that we have clearly, in the first half of the statement, Christ's own understanding that, as we have seen in the design of God's redemptive covenant, he came to save those whom the Father had given to him in the predeterminate divine council. In the second half of the statement we have the assurance that Christ will, in fact, receive freely all who come to him. Looked at from another perspective, the question may well arise as to why not all come to him. Or in other terms, who will come to him? The answer is that only those will come to whom God conveys his grace of regeneration, imparting to them the gifts of faith and repentance that Christ purchased for them in his death on the cross.

The same outcome is clear from the instance on which Christ identified himself as the good shepherd who gives his life for his sheep. His own sheep, he said, "hear his voice: and he calleth his own sheep by name, and leadeth them out" (John 10:3). The particularity of his atonement is restated in that, as the text says, when Christ discharged his redemptive assignment he knew his own sheep "by name." He died for them particularly, and he knew their names particularly because he had written their names in the book of life before the foundation of the world (Rev 13:8, 17:8). Those who do not come to Christ do not come because they will not. They will not because they cannot. They cannot because their minds are darkened and disabled as to eternal verities by the god of this world (2 Cor 4:4; 1 Cor 2:14). Those come whom the Spirit of God draws (John 6:44). To those, the prophet Jeremiah conveys the word of God as saying: "I have loved thee with an everlasting love: therefore with lovingkindness have I drawn thee" (Jer 31:3). Against the darkness and the disabilities of sin, it is said of those who come to Christ that "God, who commanded the light to shine out of darkness [at the first creation], hath shined in our hearts [at the new creation, or at the impartation of new life by God's grace of regeneration], to give the light of the knowledge of the glory of God in the face of Jesus Christ" (2 Cor 4:6).

Let us see the definitive invitation of Christ in his own words: "Come unto me, all ye that labour and are heavy laden, and I will give you rest. Take my yoke upon you, and learn of me; for I am meek and lowly in heart: and ye shall find rest unto your souls" (Matt 11:28-29). We have spoken of the search for meaning and for understanding. It is a laborious search. Souls are heavy laden from the search. Many find themselves at the end of their tether and in despair of finding any coherence of meaning and spiritual rest in this life. Many have found themselves deceived and betrayed by the falsehoods and superficialities that the world has offered them. To many, the enemy of their souls has appeared as an "angel of light," (2 Cor 11:14), only to their ultimate deception and dismay. They have said with an unknown hymn writer: "I tried the broken cisterns, Lord, / But ah! Their waters failed! / E'en as I stooped to drink they'd fled, / And mocked me as I wailed." The same writer went on to say: "O Christ, in Thee my soul has found, / And found in Thee alone, / The peace, the joy I sought so long, / The bliss till now unknown."[8] So it is with all those whom, from out of the burden of sin, the Spirit of God calls to Christ and to life eternal.

But there is reason to fear that the call of the gospel and the meaning of faith in Christ are indistinctly understood in parts of the church's theology. The theology of the New Perspective on Paul in relation to the

---

8. Anonymous. *O Christ, in Thee my soul has found.*

question of justification by faith in Christ has been brought to explicit focus by N.T. Wright. He concludes that "justification . . . is not a matter of *how someone enters the community of the true people of God*, but of *how you tell who belongs to that community*, not least in the period of time before the eschatological event itself, when the matter will become public knowledge."[9] And "'the gospel' is not an account of how people get saved. It is . . . the proclamation of the lordship of Jesus Christ. . . . Let us be quite clear. 'The gospel' is the announcement of Jesus' lordship, which works with power to bring people into the family of Abraham, now redefined around Jesus Christ and characterized solely by faith in him. 'Justification' is the doctrine which insists that all those who have this faith belong as full members of this family, on this basis and no other."[10] Expanding the notion of the lordship of Christ, Wright concludes further that people become Christian because "they come to believe the message; they join the Christian community through baptism, and begin to share in its common life and its common way of life. That is how people come into relationship with the living God."[11] "Believing in Jesus—believing that Jesus is Lord, and the [sic] God raised him from the dead—is what counts."[12] One may even be "justified without knowing it."[13]

Wright thereby stresses the lordship of Christ as a focal point of Christian belief. An effective response to this emphasis has been made by Gaffin: "Wright is emphatic that Jesus is Lord, but much less clear about how he is Savior. His presentation of Paul's gospel is at least open to being construed as follows: it's not that Jesus, because he's my Savior, is my Lord; rather, as he's my Lord, he's my Savior—in the sense that my salvation consists in my continuing allegiance to Jesus as Lord. The danger that this in its own way opens the door to moralism is hardly imaginary."[14]

What, then, are we to understand as the call of the gospel? It involves more than a bare statement that Jesus is Lord. Moreover, it involves more than a bare rational agreement that amounts to "mere belief" in Christ.[15]

9. Wright, *What Saint Paul Really Said*, 119.
10. Ibid., 133. See also ibid., 45, 60, 118.
11. Ibid., 116–17.
12. Ibid., 159.
13. Idem.
14. Gaffin, "Paul the Theologian," 125.
15. See Elliott, *Christianity and Neo-Liberalism*, 12, who refers to "the Gospel doc-

The call of the gospel is a call to repentance and faith in Christ. That was what Paul had in view in his response to the Philippian jailor. It is what Christ had in view in his call to "come unto me." Faith in Christ involves an individual's assent to what God has said as to the human condition in sin and the recognition that what God has said is true. It involves, beyond a mere statement of belief, beyond the expression of God-given faith and repentance, a commitment to Christ and a trust in the saving competence of the substitutionary sacrifice Christ has made for sin. The Westminster Catechism to which we have referred clarifies the matter: "Faith in Jesus Christ is a saving grace, whereby we receive *and rest upon him alone* for salvation, as he is offered to us in the gospel."[16] And as to repentance, which accompanies saving faith as the gift of God in communicating to the sinner the grace of regeneration, the Catechism states: "Repentance unto life is a saving grace, whereby a sinner, out of a true sense of his sin, and apprehension of the mercy of God in Christ, doth, with grief and hatred of his sin, turn from it unto God, with full purpose of, and endeavor after, new obedience."[17]

The declaration of the gospel calls upon the sinner to do what he has by nature no ability to do. He is called to repentance for sin and to faith and trust in Christ. But by reason of the inabilities of soul that characterize his fallen nature he has by himself no interest in the call of Christ and no ability to respond. Remarkably, therefore, God, by the sovereign operation of his Holy Spirit in the souls of those whom Christ has redeemed, conveys to them the graces of repentance and faith. The question that challenges our understanding of the gospel of God's grace is that of how any of those to whom the gospel is addressed can, in fact, be saved. It is part of the gospel that God gives to the sinner what he has demanded of him. Repentance and faith are the gifts of God, the gifts that Christ purchased for his people in his sacrificial death. They are "saving graces."[18] God's intervention in the souls of those he calls is clarified in the Confessional statement: "Effectual calling is the work of God's Spirit, whereby, convincing us of our sin and misery, enlightening our minds in the knowledge of Christ, and renewing our wills, he doth

---

trine of justification by faith (mere belief) in Christ alone," parenthesis in original.
16. Westminster Shorter Catechism, Question 86, italics added.
17. Ibid., Question 87.
18. Ibid., Questions 86, 87.

persuade and enable us to embrace Jesus Christ freely offered to us in the gospel."[19]

That work of God in the soul we refer to as regeneration. It is a renewing of the faculties of the soul and the conveyance to them of abilities and capacities they did not previously possess. It involves at the same time the implantation within the soul of a new *habitus*, or disposition or principle of action, that moves the sinner to turn to Christ and henceforth to endeavor after new obedience to Christ. At the moment of regeneration the individual who is the beneficiary of that grace is "delivered . . . from the power of darkness, and . . . translated . . . into the kingdom of [God's] dear Son" (Col 1:13). By that sovereign action of God the repentant sinner is "sealed with [the] Holy Spirit" (Eph 1:13), he is "baptized into one body" of Christ (1 Cor 12:13), and he is joined to Christ in a vital, spiritual, and indissoluble union (Gal 2:20).

It may be rejoined that there is difficulty in understanding how a sincere offer of the gospel accords with what we have said regarding the terms of the Covenant of Grace and, in particular, the fact that Christ died for his elect people in that he bore the penalty of their sins particularly and not the sin of all men indiscriminately. Observe, first, our Lord's lament over Jerusalem: "O Jerusalem, Jerusalem . . . how often would I have gathered thy children together, as a hen doth gather her brood under her wings, and ye would not!" (Luke 13:34). Are we to say that our Lord was not sincere in what he had said? The reality was that the people to whom Christ came would not receive him because they willed not to do so. "He came unto his own, and his own received him not" (John 1:11). "And this is the condemnation, that light is come into the world, and men loved darkness rather than light, because their deeds were evil" (John 3:19). Or as to the veracity of God, consider the apostolic declaration: "God our Saviour . . . will have all men to be saved, and to come to the knowledge of the truth" (1 Tim 2:3–4). And "the Lord is . . . not willing that any should perish, but that all should come to repentance" (2 Pet 3:9). And again, "as I live, saith the Lord God, I have no pleasure in the death of the wicked; but that the wicked turn from his way and live: turn ye, turn ye from your evil ways; for why will ye die, O house of Israel?" (Ezek 33:11). The Covenant of Grace, we have said, extends its benefits, the benefits of the death of Christ on the cross, to those who were the subjects of God's decree to elect. We have said that

19. Ibid., Question 31.

the atonement was a particular, and not an indiscriminate, atonement. Are we to say, then, that the statement of the prophet Ezekiel as to God's desire, the statement of the apostle Peter, as also Christ's lament over Jerusalem, were not reflecting a genuine sincerity on God's part? The question strikes at the heart of the free offer of the gospel.

We have spoken of "the mystery of godliness," and here we come again to the mystery involved in God's redemptive covenant. Yes, the offer of the gospel is a sincere and free offer, and all who will may respond affirmatively and be saved. But the question remains as before: who will? And the answer is the same. Only those will to whom God conveys the grace of regeneration and the gifts of saving faith and repentance. But lying behind that statement of outcomes in the world is the question and reality to which we can advert only with extreme care and humility. John Murray has judiciously struck to the heart of the issue: "God himself expresses an ardent desire for the fulfilment of certain things which he has not decreed in his inscrutable counsel to come to pass. This means that there is a will to the realization of what he has not decretively willed, a pleasure towards that which he has not been pleased to decree. This is indeed mysterious . . . God desires or has pleasure in the accomplishment of what he does not decretively will. . . . God reveals himself . . . as taking pleasure in or desiring the repentance and life of the wicked. This will of God to repentance and salvation is universalized and . . . therefore . . . there is in God a benevolent lovingkindness towards the repentance and salvation of even those whom he has not decreed to save."[20]

It is apposite to reflect finally on the statement of Isaiah the prophet: "For my thoughts are not your thoughts, neither are your ways my ways, saith the LORD. For as the heavens are higher than the earth, so are my ways higher than your ways, and my thoughts than your thoughts" (Isa 55:8–9).[21] To focus on the soteriological import of the text, or on its relevance to God's statement and provision of the way of salvation, we note that in the preceding verses God had stated that "I will make an everlasting covenant . . . even the sure mercies of David." In that, we have the messianic promise written large. The text then is stating that in the whole matter of God's design of salvation and the rescue from sin into

---

20. Murray and Stonehouse, *Free Offer of the Gospel*, 26–27.

21. The exegesis of the text is discussed at length in Vickers, *The Immediacy of God*, 148–51, taking account of the possible epistemological and soteriological interpretations of it.

which Adam's fall had plunged the race, man's possible imaginations are turned completely upside down. The issue points to what the apostle Paul spoke about convincingly when he observed that here in the whole conception of redemption we have "the mystery of Christ" (Eph 3:4).

THE COVENANT OF GRACE

The Covenant of Grace came to expression on God's part immediately our first parents had fallen into to sin. For the final time now prior to their expulsion from the garden, God met with them "in the garden in the cool of the day" (Gen 3:8). It was not a meeting in halcyon calmness and mutual holy communion as in former times. Now our first parents' love of God had turned to the terror of fear. They "hid themselves from the presence of the LORD God amongst the trees of the garden" (Gen 3:8). That is the irrationality of sin. Sin runs from God, it hates the presence of God, but there is no escape. The awareness of God implanted in the human consciousness, the *sensus deitatis*, commands the realization that God is our environment. No evasion on Adam's part could kill the conviction that now he had to do with the sovereign Lord and judge of the universe. Sin must in due time find the sinner out. It contains its own repayment, as it betrays the soul that nurtured it. Now the entailment of sin must be met, and the prospects for life that Adam's fall portended must be stated.

God had made all provision for Adam's continued life in the garden. He had planted in the midst of the garden a tree of life, the eating of whose fruit had been for Adam a sacrament. It had been an assurance to him of the promise of God that Adam would merit eternal life on condition of obedience to the law of God. The tree of life, Turretin has observed, "was a sacrament and symbol of the immortality which would have been bestowed upon Adam if he had persevered in his first state. . . . As often as he tasted its fruit, he was bound to recollect that he had life not from himself, but from God. . . . With respect to future life, it was a declarative and sealing sign of the happy life to be passed in paradise and to be changed afterwards into a heavenly life, if he had continued upright. . . . With respect to the state of grace, it was an illustrious type of the eternal happiness prepared for us in heaven; also a type of Christ himself who acquired and confers it upon us and who is therefore called 'the tree of

Biblical Foundations 45

life in the midst of the paradise of God' (Rev 2:7)"[22] Not all theologians, however, have grasped the importance of the sacramental significance of the tree of life.[23]

But now our first parents were no longer permitted to partake of that sacrament. That in itself is the starkest indicator of the results and the implications of their fall into sin. Now that Adam was expelled from the garden, "cherubims, and a flaming sword" were placed at the garden "to keep the way of the tree of life . . . lest [Adam] put forth his hand, and take also of the tree of life, and eat, and live for ever" (Gen 3: 24, 22). That prohibition was in itself an act of mercy on God's part. The intention of the text is to contemplate the possibility that Adam, following his expulsion from the garden, might attempt to partake of the fruit of the tree of life and, as the text says, improperly imagine that he could thereby "live for ever," mistakenly imagining that he would thereby gain eternal life. By doing so, on the contrary, he would have brought damnation on himself. God by his action protected Adam from that possibility, in view, it becomes clear, of the part that Adam was to play under the Covenant of Grace in the future realization of God's redemptive purposes. While Adam continued in the state of righteousness he was qualified to partake of the sacrament. Now that he had sinned, his qualification was at an end. It is of interest that the same relations apply in the present form of administration of God's Covenant of Grace. Those of God's people who come in true repentance and faith, the church admits to the sacrament of the Lord's Table. But as was true in the case of Adam, those who are under the discipline of the church by reason of unrepented sin must again be excluded from the sacrament. In both instances, whoever, as the apostle says, partakes of the sacrament "unworthily, shall be guilty of the body and blood of the Lord" (1 Cor 11:27). That realization underlines Turretin's observation that the tree of life was a type of Christ, a prevision of the true life that is found in him alone.

But God must be true to his covenant. Its implications were twofold. His justice must honor his initial promise of malediction in the event of sin, at the same time as his mercy renewed his promise of life to those he chose to redeem. On the first of those levels, the man would henceforth find his sustenance from a reluctant earth that was now

---

22. Turretin, *Institutes*, vol. 1, 581.

23. For an interpretation contrary to what we have suggested see Vos, *Biblical Theology*, 38.

cursed with "thorns and thistles" (Gen 3:18). The ordinance of work did not, of course, await the fall. Adam had at the beginning been given the mandate and responsibility to "replenish the earth, and subdue it" (Gen 1:28). But now the earth would give forth its fruit only grudgingly, and it was said to Adam that "in the sweat of thy face shalt thou eat bread" (Gen 3:19). To the woman it was said that now "in sorrow thou shalt bring forth children" (Gen 3:16). But the integrity of God's covenantal promise of life is preserved and restated in what can only be called the first statement of the gospel, the *protoevangelium*.

We observe God's address to the serpent: "I will put enmity between thee and the woman, and between thy seed and her seed; it shall bruise thy head, and thou shalt bruise his heel" (Gen 3:15). Here, in God's address to Satan who had spoken through the serpent to deceive our first parents, it is being said that a descendent of the woman would in due time come into the world and would destroy the devil and all his power. From that time on, there would be a division between a godly and an ungodly race. And from that godly race a redeemer would come. We note the clear suggestion in the text of the individuality of the "seed of the woman" in the statement that "*it*" shall bruise the head of the serpent, and the intimation that at the last time a single representative of Satan will be involved in the final destruction: "*thou* shalt bruise his heel." That projection of singularity is borne out by the explanation of the apostle in his letter to the Galatian church: "Now to Abraham and his seed were the promises made. He saith not, And to seeds, as of many; but as of one, *And to thy seed, which is Christ*" (Gal 3:16, italics added).

From Adam's fall to the coming of Christ and his completion of his redeeming work, the record of God's intervention in the history of the world in order to implement the terms of his Covenant of Grace is spread across the pages of Scripture. It is not necessary to rehearse it in detail at this point. But the history of the race quickly brings into focus the expanding reality of sin in the world and in the hearts of men. From the first son of Adam, Cain who had murdered his brother Abel, came a progeny that were both dissolute on the one hand and the recipients of God's common grace on the other. Cain's descendent, Lamech, was by his own confession a multiple murderer who also broke God's law of monogamy. But his sons by one wife developed a pastoral industry, "the father of such as dwell in tents, and of such as have cattle," and the other the musical arts, "the father of all such as handle the harp and organ."

Biblical Foundations 47

The son of Lamech's second wife developed a manufacturing industry, "an instructor of every artificer in brass and iron" (Gen 4:19–24). So it has continued throughout history. By his common grace God has developed in the world the manual and the liberal arts, and the skills of science, technology, and industry.

The significance of that early history is that within it we see, as has been said, the beginnings of the benefits of God's common grace in the world. God has continued to shower his blessings on mankind in general, notwithstanding their sin, at the same time as he has sovereignly brought to realization his promises of redemption for his people. The distinction is to be noted and preserved between God's common grace and the redemptive grace he has addressed to his own people's condition. The former is displayed in its negative and its positive aspects. Negatively, God's common grace operates as a restraint of sin. Men in general are not as sinful as they might be. Notwithstanding the evidences and events of sin and its pervasive influence in the dissolution of contemporary culture, sin is nevertheless restrained by the grace of God until it comes, at the last day and at the crack of doom, to its full expression. Then common grace will have come to an end. In the meantime, the positive expression of God's common grace is in the development of human culture.

We note also that at, and immediately following, their fall, our first parents were conscious that they were unclothed. Their nakedness was, it quickly became clear, not only or even primarily physical. Now they were denuded of all of the blessings of knowledge, holiness, and righteousness, and of the joy of knowing and communing with God in all purity that had to that time been their natural province. Now their life was suddenly darkened. They were lost now, as to any grasp of meaning and understanding of existential realities and of what God had promised as the potentialities of their initial blissful state. But their physical nakedness itself called forth the grace of God. God made for them coats of animal skin and clothed them (Gen 3:21). That action on God's part, involving as it did the death of the animals, undoubtedly pointed to what God would later institute as the necessity for animal sacrifice as an atonement for sin. But the suggestion can be made also that in God's making provision for the animal comfort of our first parents we have the beginnings of his administration of common grace. For is he not thereby saying to Adam and Eve that there is no point in their attempting to cover their sin or to provide for themselves in the manner they did with the mere leaves of a tree? God knows the needs of his creatures, and is he not saying that henceforth, as they live out their lives in the fallen and sinful world they have brought upon themselves, they will not be able to provide for themselves but will be dependent on his gracious provision for them? That is the beginning of the administration of his common grace. If the suggestion holds, we have at the very beginning, then, the clear twofold statement of God. It is by his grace that the world and all that is in it is preserved; and it is by his grace that from within the world a particular people will be redeemed to share his eternal kingdom of glory with him. It is to be understood that the first of those objectives is in order to the realization of the second. God preserves the world in order that all of those whom Christ redeemed by his death on the cross, including those still to be born, will be brought to him. We shall suggest at a later point, therefore, that God's common grace is to be understood as part of Christology, or, that is, that it is administered by God as a result of, and in the interests of, what Christ has done in redeeming his people. In another context we have said the same thing by observing that God is now eventuating all of the history of the world in the interest of his church. That, in other words, stands at the very beginning of the biblical philosophy of history.

COVENANTAL HISTORY

The cancer of sin in the world metastasized rapidly. Soon it had to be said that "God saw that the wickedness of man was great in the earth, and that every imagination of the thoughts of his heart was only evil continually" (Gen 6:5). The Noahic deluge and the new beginning that followed from it was the result. From that point on, we have a new and gradually institutionalized administration of God's Covenant of Grace. Three things are now to be maintained in focus.

First, within the patriarchal history God established his covenant with Abraham to whom he gave a threefold promise: First, the promise of a land that his descendants would inherit; second, the promise that Abraham would be the father of many nations, and that a people numberless as the stars of the heaven or the sand in the seashore would descend from him; and third, and of particular prominence, the promise that God would be God to Abraham and to his covenanted people. "In thee," God said to Abraham, "shall all families of the earth be blessed" (Gen 12:3). "I will establish my covenant between me and thee and thy seed after thee in their generations for an everlasting covenant, to be a God unto thee, and to thy seed after thee" (Gen 17:7–8). It is of particular moment that at the same time God gave to Abraham a sign and seal of the covenant in the form of circumcision (Gen 17:10). That is not to be understood as primarily a sign of national identity. It contains within it a unique spiritual significance, in that it carried with it the same conditional promises, of blessing and benediction on the one hand and curse and malediction on the other, that we have seen were inherent in God's first covenant with Adam. Again the promise of blessing and life in relation to God was attached to obedience to the law of God, and that of malediction was correspondingly attached to disobedience. (See Rom 4:11). The fact that circumcision was a blood sign signified that if the recipient of it was not faithful to the obligations assumed under the covenant, then he should be guilty of death. At the same time, the fact that God appeared to Abraham in the form of a burning lamp that passed between the animal parts that Abraham had laid out on God's instructions (Gen 15:9–18), meant that God was himself swearing an oath to Abraham that he on his part would be faithful to the covenantal promises he had made. If he were not faithful, he said, let him not be God. That remarkable fact is recalled by the writer to the Hebrews who states that God underscored his covenant to Abraham, and that to establish "the immutability of his counsel, confirmed it by an oath" (Heb 6:17).

In a highly significant sense, the Abrahamic covenant spans from its inception until the coming of Christ, who in his definitive and substitutionary sacrifice for sin paid the price for the redemption of all those who had from the beginning been conceived as the spiritual progeny of Abraham. For that reason Paul the apostle could say to the Galatians that "if ye be Christ's, then are ye Abraham's seed, and heirs according to the promise" (Gal 3:29). Within the arc of the Abrahamic covenant there nestles God's establishment of a new and fuller administration of the Covenant of Grace in the institutionalized form of his covenant with Moses. The Mosaic covenant spans from its inception to the coming of Christ. The ceremonial law under that covenantal arrangement, and the forms of temple worship and the responsibilities of the Levitical priesthood, pointed to the coming of Christ as the true High Priest who, in his death on the cross, would be both the priest who offered the sacrifice and himself the atoning offering. He was the antitype foreshadowed by the types exhibited in the ceremonial law and the Levitical priesthood.

When he made the definitive offering for sin "the veil of the temple was rent in twain from the top to the bottom" (Matt 27:51), and the way was open for all of Abraham's seed, the beneficiaries of Christ's redemption, to enter directly into the most holy place in Christ as he brings them to the throne of God the Father.

In the successive forms of administration of God's Covenant of Grace, and concurrent with the continuation of the Mosaic covenant, the covenant with David established a kingship under the theocracy of God that continued until Christ came. The kingship of David uniquely fulfills the promise that Jacob had given to his sons: "The sceptre shall not depart from Judah, nor a law-giver from between his feet, until Shiloh come" (Gen 49:10). Again in the Davidic kingship we have observable types of Christ who would come as the great King to establish his eternal kingdom in the hearts of his people. Our Lord declared his kingly authority when, in the course of a disputation with certain incredulous Jews he said: "If I with the finger of God cast out devils, no doubt the kingdom of God is come upon you" (Luke 11:20). Christ will reign until "he shall have delivered up the kingdom to God, even the Father; when he shall have put down all rule and all authority and power" (1 Cor 15:24). At that eschatological time Christ will have completed and fulfilled all of the elements of his messianic assignment, and his messianic kingship will come to an end. It remains, of course, that Christ's *essential* kingship and dominion will have no end. It is his *messianic* kingship that will, as the text has said, be surrendered to the Father. Christ at that time will have fulfilled all of the responsibilities of his messianic offices of prophet, priest, and king. He will have satisfied as the antitype that was to come all of the promises that had been projected by the anticipatory types of him that inhered in earlier forms of administration of the Covenant of Grace.

The second of the prominent features of the historic eventuation of what the Covenant of Grace contemplated was a successive narrowing of God's identification of the beneficiaries of it, a successive particularization of the channels through which its benefits were to come to effect. First, from the sons of Abraham, it was Isaac who became his heir under the covenant, and not the son of the bondmaid (Gal 4:22); and to Isaac the promise was renewed: "I will be with thee, and will bless thee; for unto thee, and to thy seed . . . I will perform the oath which I sware unto Abraham thy father." (Gen 26:3). Then from the sons of Isaac, Jacob became the heir of faith and Esau was rejected (Rom 9:13). And so the line descended through Jacob's son, Judah, to king David. God, in establishing his covenants with men at all times since the fall of our first parents, has progressively discriminated in accordance with his eternally wise and electing purposes. And so it has continued. The time would come, God promised, when the old Mosaic covenant and the Davidic kingship that succeeded him through the human dynasty he established would come to an end. Then, with the coming of Christ a new covenant would come to effect. "Behold, the days come, saith the LORD, that I will make a new covenant with the house of Israel, and with the house of Judah. . . . This shall be the covenant that I will make . . . I will put my law in their inward parts, and write it in their hearts; and will be their God, and they shall be my people" (Jer 31:31, 33).

In that covenanted outcome we see again God's discrimination. In the Covenant of Redemption that was formulated in the council of the Godhead before the foundation of the world, God, in the mandate of his eternally wise and holy will, did not elect all men as the beneficiaries of Christ's redemption. From out of the fallen host of Adam and his posterity God elected some to salvation. God's grace is discriminatory. We have already said that in our finitude we have no access to a comprehensive knowledge or understanding of the dictates of the divine will that determines and lies behind all he has done.

When we have considered the successive administrations of God's Covenant of Grace, and after taking account of God's progressive particularization among men in those administrations, a third and crowning aspect of the Covenant of Grace appears. We observe in the Old Testament record specific references to, and prophecies of, the coming of Christ as the Lord of the covenant. Of prime notice is what we have seen as the *protoevangelium*, the first statement of the gospel, of Genesis 3:15. But the Psalms and the prophets are extensive in their anticipation of Christ. Our Lord himself confirmed the Old Testament anticipation of him on more than one occasion and in more than one way. In two highly significant post-resurrection appearances he made the point. On an occasion when he ate "broiled fish and an honeycomb" with his disciples he explained to them that "these are the words which I spake unto you, while I was yet with you, that all things must be fulfilled, which were written in the law of Moses, and in the prophets, and in the psalms concerning me" (Luke 24:42, 44). Christ himself, as the Lord of the covenant, is the key to the Scriptures.

On another occasion immediately following his resurrection, our Lord walked with two of his crestfallen disciples on the road to Emmaus. In an act of self-disclosure that culminated in his taking supper with them and breaking bread that opened their eyes to his identity, Christ "beginning at Moses and all the prophets . . . expounded unto them in all the scriptures the things concerning himself" (Luke 24:27).

The Old Testament prophecies of Christ's coming are too copious to be adduced at length. They repay careful investigation. Isaiah had spoken prophetically of Christ as the "rod out of the stem of Jesse . . . a Branch . . . out of his roots" who would come (Isa 11:1). With remarkable explicitness Isaiah had prophesied that "behold, a virgin shall conceive, and bear a son, and shall call his name Immanuel" (Isa 7:14). And in the uniquely evangelical part of his prophecy, beginning at the fortieth chapter, Isaiah looks repeatedly to the coming of Christ. "Behold my servant, whom I uphold; mine elect, in whom my soul delighteth; I have put my spirit upon him: he shall bring forth judgment to the Gentiles. . . . A bruised reed shall he not break, and the smoking flax shall he not quench: he shall bring forth judgment unto truth" (Isa 42:1, 3). Isaiah's vision of the substitutionary death of Christ as the definitive sacrifice for sin is too well known to need recall at length. "He is despised and rejected of men; a man of sorrows, and acquainted with grief . . . Surely he hath borne our griefs . . . he was wounded for our transgressions, he was bruised for our iniquities . . . with his stripes we are healed." (Isa 53:3–12). As to the coming of Christ, the prophet Micah had foreseen even the place of his birth: "But thou, Bethlehem Ephratah . . . out of thee shall he come forth unto me that is to be ruler of Israel" (Micah 5:2).

BIBLICAL INSPIRATION AND AUTHORITY

We have observed in the foregoing some principal aspects of the biblical foundations for what has been said regarding the being and the covenantal decrees of God, the accomplishment of redemption by the cross of Christ, and the free offer of the gospel of salvation. We have seen that in all aspects of investigation into the meaning of reality the Scriptures provide the final locus of explanation and the criteria of truth. "In Christ," we have acknowledged from the scriptural data, "are hid all the treasures of wisdom and knowledge" (Col 2:3). The Scriptures are our only reliable source of truth and the only foundation on which we can stand. But we have already observed that such claims have been called in question.

In our concluding chapter, therefore, we shall return to a fuller discussion of the grounds on which the claims of biblical authority and reliability are based. But for purposes of what lies ahead it will be useful to anticipate briefly certain conclusions and results that are critically foundational. First, it is to be emphasized that the Holy Spirit of God is the primary or ultimate author of the Scriptures as they were given in the original autographs. Further, by virtue of God's providential preservation of the Scriptures we can say that in proper translation we have at this time the inerrant Word of God. By reason of the Holy Spirit's inspiration of the secondary human authors, we hold that the very words of the Scriptures, in all their individuality and plurality, are the words of God. The Scriptures, moreover, are self-attesting as to their veracity, reliability, and authority, and we know that the Scriptures are the Word of God because in them we hear the voice of God speaking to the human mind, heart, and conscience.

There was not, it is to be carefully maintained, an equal ultimacy between the primary and the secondary authors of the Scriptures. Rather, "holy men of God spake as they were moved [or were borne, or were carried along] by the Holy Ghost" (2 Pet 1:21). And "all scripture is given by inspiration of God [Greek: God-breathed]" (2 Tim 3:16). The inerrancy of the Scriptures is established, therefore, by their divine authorship. But the relation that existed between the primary and secondary authors has attracted varying interpretations in the history of the church. A principal question that has exercised the minds of the theologians has concerned the extent to which it can be said that an analogy or a parallel exists between the divine and human natures of Christ and the divine and human elements of the Scriptures. It is on precisely that ground that much dispute has existed in the relevant literature and on which prominent claims and counterclaims have been made in recent times. We shall bring that dispute briefly under review.

On the basis of our commitment to a well-established doctrine of Scripture, we turn immediately in the following chapter to the central question of the meaning and message of the cross.

3

The Cross: Its Meaning and Message

THE PROBLEM OF OUR time, we said in our opening chapter, is the problem of man. The doctrine of man, his being, nature, covenantal obligations, sin, and prospective destiny, are addressed under the heading of biblical anthropology. It tells us how the human story began. Our first parent came from the hands of a Creator-God; at the beginning he walked with God "in the garden in the cool of the day" (Gen 3:8); and he was constituted under God as a prophet, priest, and king. He was mandated to investigate and know and understand and dedicate back to the glory of God all the discoverable aspects of the reality-environment in which he came to self-consciousness. In the very act of self-awareness Adam was aware of God. For him to *be* was to *know*. He was created in a state of knowledge, holiness, and righteousness. He was constitutively holy, and as the image of God it was possible for him not to fall. But in his state of finitude he was mutable, defectible and, as we have already seen, the Scriptures report Adam's repudiation of his covenantal obligations to God and they explain what that has involved for all his natural posterity.

Now as we consider directly the cross of Christ, the human condition comes prominently to focus. For it was in order to address the human condition that Christ came into the world. The redemption for sinners that was ordained in the eternal and predeterminate council of God was now to come to full effect. But what are we to say, and what does the world in general say, of the cross of Christ? It stands, we have said, as the watershed of history. Its divine transaction, coming to predestined effect at the culmination of prophetic anticipation, spoke definitively to the human condition and the perplexities that had plagued it since Adam's dereliction. But what are we to say is the *meaning* of the cross? Poets have exhausted vocabularies in their reach for meaning as they have "surveyed the wondrous cross."[1] Philosophers have alternatively scorned and gloried in what they have conjured as the significance of the cross. Theologians have spun their varied and conflicting theories. And the common man has too often been left to wonder how the inspired record of the cross is to be read. The distinctive marks of the watershed of history have been blurred in the annals of interpretation.

Consider, then, the fact of the cross. But we pause. For here, paramount among all instances of search for meaning, it is necessary to reflect on the meaning of factness itself. What, in short, is the fact of the cross we set out to discuss and why, if that fact is properly perceived and construed, has the cross bequeathed its significance to the centuries that followed? When Leslie Weatherhead, a prominent twentieth-century British theologian, wrote his *A Plain Man Looks at the Cross*, he presented his work as "an attempt to explain, in simple language for the modern man, the significance of the death of Christ."[2] But the question at issue at the end of Weatherhead's plain man looking at the cross is: What did the plain man *see* in the cross? Our own conclusion will be that the Scriptures not only provide a statement of the *fact* of the cross, but beyond that, or more properly associated with that, they declare the *meaning* of the fact of the cross. For it is necessary to see that on all levels of cognition it is the *meaning* of the fact that gives the fact its factness. Facticity is dependent on meaning.

That is clear from the following. We contemplate Jesus Christ dying on Golgotha's gibbet and we ask: What is the fact we are witnessing? For some observers the fact is that there we see a man, an imposter and deceiver, reaping the just deserts of his misguided and misspent, disastrous life. For others, undoubtedly few, the fact is that there on the cross is the incarnate Son of God dying in the place of sinners. What, then, is the fact? The fact, for the respective observers, is inseparable from, and it is itself determined by, the meaning imported into it, or the meaning it is conceived to project. Or more properly, the fact in that instance is established by the meaning announced by the Word of God as constituting it. It is the remarkable competence of the Scriptures that in them we have not only a clear record of the facts that God has eventuated in the history of his providence and redemption, but also the meaning of the facts. In that, of course, we have simply a statement of what lies at the base of

1. Watts, *When I survey the wondrous cross*, 252.
2. Weatherhead, *A Plain Man Looks at the Cross*.

every attempt to establish a truly Reformed theological apologetic. For that necessarily recognizes that all the facts of created reality and history are God's facts, and that our task at the level of cognition is not to make an original interpretation of the facts but to make a *re*interpretation of the *pre*interpretation that God has already given.[3] There are not, that is to say, any "brute facts" that for the Christian interpreter form the basis of knowledge. There are no brute facts that provide ultimate epistemological data.

Now the significance and application of what has been said require us to see what the scriptural revelation lays before us as the meaning and the message of the cross of Christ. The following discussion will make some preliminary suggestions to that effect by asking, first, what are we to say of the Person of Jesus Christ who went to the cross for us; second, why did he go to the cross; and third, who are the beneficiaries of the cross and what are the benefits which, by virtue of the cross, accrue to them?

THE INCARNATE CHRIST

It is not necessary to rehearse at length the controversies in the early church that preceded the christological settlement at the Council of Chalcedon in the year 451 AD. The Arians had argued that Jesus Christ was a created entity who was not eternally God in his own right. He was not, they argued, autotheotic. The Sabellians attempted to controvert the biblical revelation that God exists as a trinity of Persons, "the same in substance, equal in power and glory."[4] They argued that the Son and the Holy Spirit were only emanations of the one God, not existing eternally within the Godhead as distinguishable Persons. After the rigorous defense of the truth by the worthy Athanasius in the fourth century following the Council of Nicea in 324, and on through the Councils of Constantinople in 381 and Ephesus in 431 to Chalcedon in 451, the church preserved the biblical revelation. Jesus Christ was the eternal Son of God who, as Chalcedon stated it, took into union with

---

3. Van Til has made the same point in his reference to the "Adamic consciousness" in which our first parent sought to be "receptively reconstructive" of God's revelation, "a reinterpreter of the interpretation of God," while fallen man seeks to be "creatively constructive." Van Til observes further regarding the "regenerate consciousness" that it "has *in principle* been restored to the position of the Adamic consciousness" and seeks "to be receptively reconstructive once more." *Defense of the Faith*, 48–49.

4. Westminster Shorter Catechism, Question 6.

his divine nature a true human nature, and in his Person the two natures were joined in union "without confusion, without change, without division, and without separation."⁵

Who is it, then, that we see dying there as we contemplate the cross? It is the eternal Son of God. The mystery startles us. We cannot plumb the depth of its meaning. The one dying on the cross was not always Jesus Christ. He came from the eternal bosom of the Father to *become* Jesus Christ for our redemption. "God . . . *gave* his son" (John 3:16). In the fullness of time he "*sent* forth his Son" (Gal 4:4). God "loved us and *sent* his Son to be the propitiation for our sins" (1 John 4:10). From the eternal council of the Godhead the Son came into the world to become man to redeem fallen men and bring them back to God, to become *Jesus*, his human name, and to be the *Christ*, the promised and anointed One, the Messiah, the promise of whose coming had lighted the pages of the Old Testament. In "the law of Moses, and in the prophets, and in the psalms" (Luke 24:44) we see Jesus Christ, the Son of God, set clearly before us.

But there is mystery in the death of the Son of God, as there is mystery in his incarnation, his coming into the world. For how can it be said that the Son of God died? The man Jesus Christ died, but he died in his human nature. That is the locus of mystery. He died as man for the people whom God the Father had given him to redeem. "Thine they were, and thou gavest them me," Christ spoke back to the Father in his high priestly prayer (John 17:6). Jesus Christ, when he was in this world, was truly man. Sin had entered the world in human nature, and if any from among the fallen progeny of Adam were to be redeemed, the penalty for sin must be paid in human nature. But we hold to the biblical revelation that Jesus Christ, though he was truly man, was not a human person. He was, he remained, and he continues to be, a divine Person. Nor can it be said, as we have already noted, that he was a divine-human person, in the sense that in some respect that then remained to be explained the divine and human natures were commingled. In that case, it could not be said that he was either uniquely divine or uniquely human. Because we hold that Christ was, and is, a divine Person, not a human

---

5. The Christological settlement as stated at Chalcedon can be inspected in numerous histories of theology. See for example, Shedd, *History of Christian Doctrine*, vol.1, 399–408; Van Til, *Defense of the Faith*, 16; Turretin, *Institutes*, vol. 2, 306–10; Bavinck, *Reformed Dogmatics, Volume 3*, 253–59.

person, it has to be said that the divine nature was the essential locus of his personhood.

The late nineteenth-century Reformed theologian at Union Theological Seminary, W. G. T. Shedd, observed judiciously in that connection: "When these two natures are *united* in one theanthropic person, as they are in the incarnation, the divine determines and controls the human, not the human the divine."[6] Shedd had previously stated that "it is the divine nature, not the human nature, which is the base of Christ's person."[7] Further, "the divine nature constantly supports the human nature under all the temptations to sin that are presented to it. . . . It deserts the humanity so that it may suffer for the atonement of sin, but it never deserts the humanity so that it may fall into sin itself."[8]

The humanity and the divinity of Christ are declared by our Lord himself in his statement to Mary Magdalene immediately following his resurrection: "Go to my brethren, and say unto them, I ascend unto *my Father*, and your Father; and to *my God*, and your God" (John 20:17, italics added). In his commentary on Paul's second epistle to the Corinthians, Charles Hodge observes that "Jesus Christ is a designation of the . . . historical person . . . to whom God stood in the relation at once of *God* and *Father*. Our Lord had a dependent [human] nature to which God stood in the relation of God, and a divine nature to which He stood in the relation of Father."[9]

We do well, then, to contemplate the mystery of the incarnation of Christ, cognizable as that is in its several dimensions. First, we acknowledge the mystery that he who created time as a mode of finite existence should himself have entered into time and made himself subject to the process of time that he had created. In doing so, he took to himself a created, finite, temporal human nature, in human body and with all the properties and capacities of human soul, yet without sin. He continues in that human nature, body and soul, for all eternity, and in it he discharges his heavenly high priestly office for the benefit of those whom

---

6. Shedd, *Dogmatic Theology*, vol. 2, 332.
7. Ibid., 269.
8. Ibid., 335.
9. Hodge, C. *II Corinthians*, 653, italics added. I am indebted for this reference to Philip Edgcumbe Hughes, *Second Corinthians*, 10. We say regarding our Lord, the second Person of the Godhead, that as to his nature he is autotheotic, while as to his Person he is of the Father. See Berkhof, *Systematic Theology*, 94, cited in chapter 2 above.

he redeemed.[10] In his incarnation, in taking human nature into union with his divine nature, there was no commingling of the properties of the respective natures, no commingling of the eternal and the temporal.[11] The mystery of the incarnation of Christ requires it to be said that in his personhood he was not *monophysite*, of only one nature, and he was not *monothelite*, of only one will. There were, and there remain in Christ, both a divine will and a human will, both a divine mind and a human mind, and both a divine and a human capacity for emotion and affection. When he came into the world he did not in any sense surrender or lay aside his eternal glory. It is true that in the discharge of his messianic-redemptive assignment he laid aside the *insignia* or the *signs* of his glory.[12] But while he remained the eternal Son of God, there dwelt in him "the fulness of the Godhead bodily" (Col 2:9). He continued in total possession of the full essence of the Godhead, in all holy attributes, communicable and incommunicable. When he was in this world he was, as to his divine nature, both in this world and with the Father in heaven (John 3:13), while as to both his divine and his human natures he was in the world that he himself had spoken into existence.

Second, the very act of his incarnation contains its miracle and mystery. Reflect for a moment on the status of the virgin Mary who was honored to be the mother of our Lord. In the fact that she was the daughter of our first parent, Adam, there devolved to her the same fallenness of nature that Adam's dereliction bequeathed to all his posterity. "The covenant being made with Adam," the Westminster Shorter catechism states, "not only for himself, but for his posterity, all mankind, descending from him by ordinary generation, sinned in him, and fell with him in his first transgression."[13] Mary, in short, was the subject of the same transmission of fallen nature that devolved on and to all of Adam's posterity. The miracle of the incarnation of Christ is therefore twofold.

---

10. As to Christ's continued heavenly existence in his glorified human body, Hodge has observed insightfully that though he met with, and ate with, his disciples in this world following his resurrection, "He did not assume his permanent pneumatic state until his ascension.... His body... then assumed the state adapted to its condition in heaven." Hodge, *II Corinthians*, 351.

11. See Van Til, *Defense of the Faith*, 16–17.

12. While that is so, the miracles that Christ performed were designed to attest his deity.

13. Westminster Shorter Catechism, Question 16.

First, we reflect on the prophecy and promise of Isaiah that "a virgin shall conceive, and bear a son" (Isa 7:14), and we note that the gospel of Matthew refers to "Mary, *of whom* was born Jesus" (Matt 1:16). We are arrested by the "of whom," indicating that our Lord was born of the substance of the woman. In the divine act of incarnation it was not the case that the Spirit of God, independently of the body of Mary, created a fetus for implantation in the womb of the virgin. The child was born of the substance of Mary, by reason of the Holy Spirit's miraculous impregnation of the egg of the mother. There occurred, that is, a genuine transmission of human nature, though, as we shall observe further, that human nature was without sin.

But the first aspect of the miracle that engages our attention is that by the action of God the entailment of sin that otherwise characterized Mary in her own human condition was broken. No fallen and sinful nature was transmitted. It is stated in the words of the angel to Mary that "the Holy Ghost shall come upon thee, and the power of the Highest shall overshadow thee" (Luke 1:35). Miracle and mystery as it is, on that unique occasion and for that unique purpose, the mother of our Lord was cleansed of the entailment of sin, and the angel went on to say: "Therefore also that holy thing which shall be born of thee shall be called the Son of God." We note the "also" in the words of the angel. As a result, the child that was born was "holy." He was the sinless Son of God. And then secondly, involved in the miracle of the incarnation was, at the same time, the action of conception by the Holy Spirit that created the Christ child in the womb of the mother.[14]

Though mystery abounds, it is clear from the biblical data that, as has already been said, our Lord as he was in this world was a divine Person and not a human person. But in the light of that reality it is necessary to reflect further on the manner and the outcome of his incarnation. It is true that at the moment of fertilization in the course of conception that establishes a human fetus, a *person* thereby comes to existence.[15] (In fact, it is the reality of that emergence of personhood that argues forcibly against abortion that has become widely fashionable in

---

14. A useful discussion of "The historicity of Jesus' virginal conception" is contained in Reymond, *New Systematic Theology*, 547–52. See also Bavinck, *Reformed Dogmatics*, vol. 3, 253–59.

15. I am indebted for discussion of this matter to Dr. Lachlan Dunjey of *Medicine with Morality*, Perth, Western Australia. See www.medicinewithmorality.org.au.

contemporary cultures). What is to be said, then, of the fetus that was carried in the womb of the virgin? It follows that we must have regard to the fact that at that point a divine Person had entered into the world. The union of the divine and human natures did not wait until the virgin had carried the fetus to term. The mystery is thereby established that at fertilization the Son of God had come into the world.[16]

But we ask again: Who was it that went to the cross for our redemption? We have seen that it was the eternal Son of God who died in his human nature. But we hold to the biblical data again and state that it was the Lord Jesus Christ in his Person who died for us. True, he died, as has been said, in his human nature. But we hold that it is the *Person* of Christ who thus became our sinless redeemer, and it is to the *Person* of Christ that we look for salvation. It would be a mistake of unacceptable magnitude to suggest, as appears to have been the case in parts of medieval theology, that "Christ is mediator only according to his human nature."[17] As it is Christ in his Person who is our redeemer, so it is Christ in his Person, in full possession of his divine and his human natures, who now sits at the right hand of God and discharges his heavenly high-priestly, intercessory office on behalf of those he redeemed.

But finally, we ask again, who is it we see on the cross for us? It is the Son of God who, by reason that he fulfilled the law of God perfectly for us, was *qualified* to die for us by reason that he, as the "captain of [our] salvation," had been made "*perfect through sufferings*" (Heb 2:10). Philip Edgcumbe Hughes has summarized the issue in his valuable commentary by saying: "It is fitting that our Redeemer should have been *made perfect through suffering*: first, because his completely victorious suffering of temptation of every kind (Heb 4:15) was essential to his achievement of that perfection which *qualified* him to offer himself on the cross as the spotless Lamb of God in the place of sinners (1 Pet 1:18f; 3:18)."[18]

Redemption was accomplished, that is, by the sinless, spotless, and impeccable[19] Son of God who gave himself for us in his human nature

---

16. John Owen has made the same point in his work on *Christologia, or the Person of Christ* (1679), 45. Regarding the human nature of our Lord, Owen refers to "its assumption into personal union with the Son of God, *in the first instance of its conception*," italics added.

17. See Trueman, *Minority Report*, 33–34, and references there cited.

18. Hughes, *Hebrews*, 100, italics of "qualified" added.

19. See Vickers, *The Immediacy of God*, 131–34, for a discussion of the impeccability of Christ.

on the cross. Thus the apostle could clinch his argument for the substitutionary sacrifice of Christ: "God for our sake . . . made him to be sin who knew no sin, so that in him we might become the righteousness of God" (2 Cor 5:21, ESV).

WHY THE CROSS?

The "why" of the cross harks back, beyond the implication for all humanity of the dereliction of our first parents from the obligations of the creation covenant, to the predeterminate council of the Godhead before the foundation of the world. It is not necessary to recall at this point all that has been said regarding Adam's created status and the state of sin into which he fell. But it was the exigency of sin that occasioned, in the vision of God, the necessity of the cross. By reason of the moral inability of Adam's posterity, the divine objective of redemption necessitated the coming into the world of a substitute redeemer. We must now look briefly at what that involved.

When we have said that the meaning of the cross harks back, beyond the reality and the fact and significance of Adam's fall, to the predeterminate council of the Godhead, we are conscious of the mystery before which we stand. If we may speak with humility and with extreme care, we may say that here we are aware of the problem of eternity. The prince of God's creation now having fallen and become subject to the penalty contemplated in the probation in which God established Adam (Gen 2:16–17, "in the day that thou eatest thereof [the forbidden fruit] thou shalt surely die"), how, if at all, could divine action be taken to bring men back to reconciliation and reunion with God? It was not necessary, of course, that God in his eternal wisdom and justice should take any such action at all. It is in no sense possible to say that any necessity rested upon God to redeem Adam or any of his fallen posterity from the curse of sin. The justice of God would have been fully vindicated if he had left all men to perish in the death and eternal perdition that Adam's sin had warranted.

But at precisely that point God's justice, informed by his love for his creation and for a particular people he contemplated as sharing an eternal kingdom of glory with him, was met by his mercy. A Covenant of Grace was directed to the redemption of sinners. God's grace was directed to their guilt, and his mercy was directed to the state of misery in which they would otherwise have been eternally bound. An elect people would be redeemed. A way would be established whereby "the works of the devil" (1 John 3:8) would be destroyed, and, moreover, the One who would come in order to accomplish that would "destroy him that had the power of death, that is, the devil" (Heb 2:14). What is being said is that while no necessity rested upon God to institute a process of redemption for any who had sinned, nevertheless a decision having been made in divine council to institute redemption, the problem remained as to how that was to be accomplished.

A variety of answers have been given in the history of the church. Some have said that the sending of the Son of God into the world was only a "hypothetical necessity." That is, there could well have been other ways in which God could have saved certain people from their prospective eternal perdition. It was only the case, it has then been claimed, that for reasons that cannot be plumbed, God decided to effect salvation by sending his Son. The well-known evangelical scholar, Arthur W. Pink, for example, in his otherwise valuable work, has argued to that effect against any claim that the coming of the Son of God into the world was absolutely necessary. "To say that the all-wise God Himself could find no other way of saving sinners, consistently with His holiness and justice, than the one He has, is highly presumptuous. To declare that Omniscience was helpless, that God was obliged to adopt the means which he did, is perilously nigh unto blasphemy."[20]

Against such claims, however, the following is to be said. While there was no necessity laid upon God to redeem, nevertheless the decision to redeem having been made, it was absolutely necessary that redemption should be accomplished in the manner in which the eternal council of the Godhead declared. It was absolutely necessary, that is, that redemption should be accomplished by the cross of Christ. John Murray, the prominent mid-twentieth-century Reformed theologian, has referred judiciously to what he states as the "consequent absolute necessity" of the atonement of Christ as the substitute for sinners.[21] The justly-famed seventeenth-century Reformed scholar, FrancisTurretin, similarly raises the question: "Was it necessary for Christ to make satisfaction to divine justice for us? We affirm against the Socinians."[22] There was no other way, that is, by which redemption could be accomplished.

---

20. Pink, *Satisfaction of Christ*, 33.
21. Murray, *Redemption*, 16.
22. Turretin, *Institutes*, vol. 2, 417–426.

In the wisdom of God in the institution of redemption, "mercy and truth are met together; righteousness and peace have kissed each other" (Ps 85:10). God's justice is satisfied in the work of his Son as the substitute for sinners. God's righteousness is satisfied in order that "he might be just, and the justifier of him which believeth in Jesus" (Rom 3:26).

The conclusion therefore follows: It was absolutely necessary that in vindication of the justice and righteousness of God his law should be kept and honored. Further, as the law had been broken in human nature with the entrance of sin into the world at Adam's fall, it was necessary that the law should be kept in human nature. It was that which the Son of God came to do on our behalf. There was no other who could do and achieve what was required. No mere man could satisfy the penalty for the sins of man. Every man was condemned for his own sin that warranted eternal damnation. Only the Second Person of the Godhead could do what was necessary, by assuming sinless human nature to himself, and in that sinless nature keeping the law perfectly on behalf of those he came to redeem. In sending his Son into the world God has himself done what he required in order that his divine justice and love should be vindicated.

Moreover, an important dimension of what is at issue has been clearly stated by Paul the apostle: "Ye are not your own . . . ye are bought with a price" (1 Cor 6:19-20); and again: "Ye are bought with a price; be not ye the servants of men" (1 Cor 7:23). The fact situation is that because Christ has paid the price of our redemption, those whom he thereby purchased are his property. For that reason it can be said that whereas once the sinner was the slave of Satan and sin, now he is enslaved to Christ. His slavery to Christ is his newfound freedom. Realizing that the redeemed are the property of the redeemer, it is doubly inconceivable that any mere man could have provided a redemption for others.

But the justice of God required not only that the law should be kept and honored, but that the penalty for having broken the law should be paid to the full. Why then was the cross also necessary? It was necessary that Christ should do in that respect precisely what was accomplished on the cross. The prophet of old had already supplied the answer: "Surely he hath borne our griefs, and carried our sorrows . . . he was wounded for our transgressions, he was bruised for our iniquities: the chastisement of our peace was upon him; and with his stripes we are healed" (Isa 53:4-5). Only a sinless redeemer, who had no sin of his own for which to account, could be the substitute for sinners and pay the price of sin. "There was no other good enough," the hymn writer has said, "to pay the price of sin, / he only could unlock the gate of heav'n and let us in."[23] Well might sinners exclaim with the apostle, "thanks be unto God for his unspeakable gift" (2 Cor 9:15).

We shall refer in a moment to the benefits that accrue from the cross. But we note immediately an important result or implication of what it was that Christ did for his people on the cross. What was the import, so far as our salvation is concerned, of the transaction between the Father and the Son when Christ died his substitutionary death for us? We are arrested by his cry of dereliction: "My God, my God, why hast thou forsaken me?" (Matt 27:46). We here, if ever, stand on holy ground. What issued in the moment when time and eternity met as had never been instanced before? But this we can say: We are assisted in our understanding by our Lord's expiring words: "It is finished" (John 19:30). He had used the same words in his high priestly prayer on the preceding evening. "I have finished the work which thou gavest me to do" (John 17:4). He had rightly made that statement because of his determination to accomplish on the following day what it was he came into the world to do, and because the outcome of his final act of redemption, as well as the process he knew it would take and his willing acceptance of its course, was clearly before his eyes. Now that he had paid on the cross his substitute penalty for our sin, his work of redemption was finished. God's justice had been satisfied. His wrath against us by reason of our sin had been appeased. In the transaction on the cross, Christ was both the expiation for our sin and the propitiation of God's wrath against our sin. By expiation it is meant that the guilt of our sin was wiped away. Expiation is addressed to our guilt. It has a manward aspect. Propitiation, on the other hand, is directed to God's wrath (1 John 2:2, 4:10; Rom 3:25; Heb 2:17). By propitiation his wrath is appeased.

In that connection it is necessary to hold clearly in mind what is intended by the statement that in his death Christ bore the guilt of our sin. For what is to be understood as the meaning of guilt? In the broadest of terms, guilt is unfulfilled obligations. But guilt, defined in those terms, is to be understood in both its subjective and its objective connotations. By subjective guilt we mean the consciousness that grips the soul when it is recognized that a certain obligation has not been met. It then comes

---

23. Alexander, *There Is a Green Hill Far Away*, 256.

to consciousness as a sense of self-condemnation. Such a subjective expression of guilt may occur simply because one has failed to act in accordance with some self-established moral criteria. Indeed, those who have no understanding of the law of God and will have nothing to do with it, do generally live according to some such criteria. Those criteria may be defined by an individual for himself, or they may be copied from what generally informs his cultural milieu. But here we are concerned with guilt in relation to the law of God.

When we have in view the imputation of the sinner's guilt to Christ, we are not contemplating guilt in its subjective expression. We have in view the objective fact that by reason of their actions of sin, all individuals have failed to satisfy, or to live in accordance with, their obligations to God by reason of the covenant in which Adam, their representative head, was established on their behalf. Christ bore the objective guilt of unfulfilled obligations to God. He fulfilled those obligations on behalf of the people he came to save. He therein did for them what they were obligated to do but which, because of their state in sin, they were unable to do for themselves.

By reason of the propitiation that Christ provided in his death, by reason that the wrath of God against us because of our sin has been appeased, it can be said that "we have peace with God through our Lord Jesus Christ" (Rom 5:1). The clamor and torture of subjective guilt is dealt with and the calmness of reconciliation with God exists in the soul. God is now at peace with us. There is, for the Christian believer, a "peace of God which passes understanding" and "keeps the Christians' hearts and minds" (compare Philippians 4:7). The reference there is to the highly valuable subjective peace that accrues to the believer by reason of his relation to God and the sanctifying ministry of the Holy Spirit of God to him. But that subjective peace is not what is primarily intended in Romans 5:1. What is at issue there, as has been said, is the fact that as a result of the redeeming work of Christ, God is now at peace with his people.

We recall the fact of the reciprocal imputation that is inherent in the work of Christ on the cross. The guilt of our sin was imputed to Christ and his righteousness was imputed to us. Because Christ "bore our sins in his own body on the tree" (1 Pet 2:24), God now looks upon us as though we ourselves had paid the penalty for sin. And because Christ discharged for us our obligation to obey God's law perfectly, God now looks on us as though we had ourselves kept the law. That is the remarkable outcome of the redemption that Christ accomplished for us. It is not wide of the mark to say that because God saw his own people in Christ as Christ performed his redemptive mission on their behalf, all that happened to Christ happened to us who belong to him. When Christ died, we died. The apostle therefore exults: "Our old man is crucified with him [Christ]" (Rom. 6:6), and "I am crucified with Christ: nevertheless I live; yet not I, but Christ liveth in me; and the life which I now live in the flesh I live by the faith of the Son of God, who loved me, and gave himself for me" (Gal 2:20).

The apostle again makes his point in other terms. To the Galatian Christians he argued that "they that are Christ's have crucified the flesh with the affections and lusts" (Gal 5:24). That crucifixion occurred when the believer was "crucified with Christ" (Gal 2:20; Rom 6:6). It is said in that same chapter of the letter to the Galatians that there is an on-going war within the Christian: "The flesh lusteth against the Spirit, and the Spirit against the flesh" (Gal 5:17). We note the upper case "S" in the text. The statement has to do with the progressive sanctifying work of the Holy Spirit in the life of the believer. The former statement (Gal 5:24) reminds the Christian of the status he has been granted by reason of his union with Christ, in the light of which he is to cultivate the fruit of the Spirit that is referred to there. As the following text states: "If we live in the Spirit, let us also walk in the Spirit" (Gal 5:25).

We have asked, Why the cross? And we have answered that the cross was absolutely necessary because of sin that had in some way to be dealt with if reconciliation with God was to be reestablished for sinners. But we return for a moment to the *protoevangelium* in Genesis 3:15, where we saw the first promise that in due course was more fully declared in the cross of Christ. God had said to Adam: "Cursed is the ground for thy sake" (Gen 3:17). We have seen the meaning of the curse in the fact that the ground would henceforth give its fruits only grudgingly and that Adam would eat of the fruit, as the text says, "in the sweat of thy face" (Gen 3:19). But now more is involved. As a result of sin "the whole creation groaneth and travaileth in pain" (Rom 8:22). As a result of Adam's fall, sin invaded the universe, and all aspects of God's creation have felt its effects. What, then, in relation to that has the obedience of Christ in his death on the cross accomplished? By his death, sin is being cleansed from the universe, and as a result, in God's appointed time we shall see "a new heaven and a new earth" (Rev 21:1). Our minds are focused, therefore, on what must be called the cosmic significance of the death of Christ. As a result of that cosmic significance, the work of Christ was done in order that "in the dispensation of the fulness of times he [God] might gather together in one all things in Christ, both which are in heaven, and which are on earth; even in him" (Eph 1:10). And "then cometh the end, when he [Christ] shall have delivered up the kingdom to God, even the Father; when he shall have put down all rule and all authority and all power" (1 Cor 15:24).

The cosmic significance of Christ, Paul is saying, involves expansive realities. Christ, by his work of redemption that has cleansed the universe of sin, makes possible God's ultimate establishment of the new heaven and the new earth. When Paul said that God will "gather together in one all things in Christ" he used a Greek word that contains a prefix that conveys the sense of "again," or "by way of recapitulation." In Christ all things will be gathered together "again." The implication is that all things were subject to disruption and decay by reason of Adam's fall. Not only was man himself subject to the disabilities, the deprivation and depravation, that sin introduced. A generalized and universal disruption and decay occurred. "The creature [creation] was made subject to vanity . . . [but] the creature [creation] itself also shall be delivered from the bondage of corruption [decay] . . . For we know that the whole creation groaneth and travaileth" (Rom 8:20–22). The apostolic statement at that point is that all things will again be restored to their primeval harmony, goodness, and beauty, and that by reason of the work of Christ that surpassing, glorious eschatological terminus will be realized.

Why the Cross? Because in the cross there comes to convergent effect all that God purposed before the foundation of the world as to both the redemption of a chosen people for himself and the full eventual realization of an eternal kingdom of glory that they would share with him. We may look, therefore, behind the announced purpose of God in the Covenant of Redemption that was consummated in the cross and contemplate larger divine objectives. Those objectives are the demonstration of God's own glory and the glory of his own Son in all things, in heaven and earth, in the one by the "elect angels" (1 Tim 5:21) and by the "great cloud of witnesses" (Heb 12:1), the saints who have gone before us, and in the other by those whom by his redeeming grace he has joined to himself in Christ.

We have suggested, as Martyn Lloyd-Jones put it effectively, that "the preaching of the cross, the preaching of the death of the Lord Jesus Christ on that cross is the very heart and centre of the Christian gospel and the Christian message."[24] At the cross we come to the very climax of our Lord's redemptive mission and ministry. He came "to give his life a ransom for many" (Mark 10:45). At the end of the Galilee ministry, knowing that the time of his death approached, "he stedfastly set his face to go to Jerusalem" (Luke 9:51). For this cause he came into the world and he must fulfill the terms of his redemptive assignment. Well has the apostle responded: "God forbid that I should glory, save in the cross of our Lord Jesus Christ, by whom the world is crucified unto me, and I unto the world" (Gal 6:14). And when the same apostle came to the Gentile city of Corinth, he came, he said, "determined not to know any thing among you, save Jesus Christ, and him crucified" (1 Cor 2:2).

It has been said by some theologians that the reference to the cross of Christ is to be understood in a synecdochical sense. Synecdoche is a figure of speech in which a part of a certain referent is put for the whole, or the whole is put for the part. Theologians who take references to the cross of Christ as being synecdochical argue, then, that the reference to the cross should be taken to refer to Christ's redemptive work in its entirety, and that it should bring that entire work and its completion into view. That means, for example, that references to the cross should bring into view the completion of Christ's work as it was culminated in his resurrection and ascension and his session at the right hand of the Father in the place of authority. Richard Gaffin, for example, has oriented his view of the redemptive work of Christ on his resurrection and what he sees as its salvific implications. He does that by claiming that Christ's resurrection is to be understood as his own redemption, justification, adoption, and sanctification.[25] Given that orientation, Gaffin goes on to state that "not justification by faith but union with the resurrected Christ by faith . . . is the central motif of Paul's applied soteriology."[26] In Gaffin's theology, such claims lead to a diminishing of what has been referred to historically as the *ordo salutis*, or the order of application of redemption, whereby the Holy Spirit applies to the believer the benefits of the redemption that Christ accomplished. For Gaffin, the redemption,

---

24. Lloyd-Jones, *The Cross*, 18.
25. Gaffin, *Resurrection*, 114–27. See also Gaffin, *By Faith, Not By Sight*, 43–52.
26. Gaffin, *Resurrection*, 132.

justification, adoption, and sanctification of the believer are what they are because he shares in the redemption, justification, adoption, and sanctification that Christ accomplished for himself. The danger exists in that scheme of things that the work of the Holy Spirit in the discharge of his redemptive office, his progressive application of the benefits of Christ's redemption to those he redeemed, is diminished.

What we have seen as the synecdochical view of the cross of Christ is not, of course, completely without value and significance. But there is reason to conclude that when the cross of Christ is in view what must come to prominence is that there on the cross our Lord did, in fact, pay the penalty for sin that rescued his people from eternal death and from the misery of their prospective eternal perdition. From the death of Christ and the faithfulness with which, in his death, he discharged his redemptive assignment flows the significance of all the other aspects of his saving work. For it was on the cross that Christ uttered, before he committed his spirit to the Father: "It is finished." In his death he provided a "ransom for many" (Matt 20:28). In his death, as the hymn writer has said, he "paid the price of sin." From his death on the cross there radiates the meaning of all of the aspects of his redemptive work that he had been sent by the Father to do, and the meaning of the heavenly high priestly office he now discharges in the interests of those he redeemed.

"Why the Cross?" we have asked. Before we look more directly in the following section at the benefits and the beneficiaries of the cross of Christ, let us observe the manner in which Augustus Toplady, the prominent hymn writer of the eighteenth-century evangelical awakening, answered the question as he spoke of the cross: "Nothing in my hand I bring, / simply to thy cross I cling; / naked, come to thee for dress; / helpless look to thee for grace; / *foul, I to the Fountain fly; / wash me, Savior, or I die.*"[27] Toplady reflects the summary of the apostle John who strikes to the heart of the matter when he declares that "the blood of Jesus Christ cleanseth us from all sin" (1 John 1:7). The cross of Christ is the refuge for sinners in the distress of sin, and for the saints in their stumbling obedience and in the pressure of temptation to sin. Christ, Paul said to the Colossians, has "made peace through the blood of his cross" (Col 1:20).

---

27. Toplady, *Rock of Ages*, 499, italics added.

THE BENEFITS OF THE CROSS

It is part of the theological genius of John Calvin that he elaborated the threefold office of Christ as prophet, priest, and king.[28] In our present context of the meaning of the cross of Christ, his office as priest comes particularly to focus. In discharging that office, Christ was the antitype of the Levitical priesthood that was an integral part of the earlier form of administration of the Covenant of Grace. The difference is patent in the pages of Scripture. Christ was not only the priest who administered the definitive offering for sin, but he was himself the offering, the sacrifice to "satisfy divine justice, and reconcile us to God."[29] "The Son of God," the apostle declared, "gave *himself* for me" (Gal 2:20). It was not by "the blood of goats and calves" that Christ submitted an offering for sin, "but by his own blood" (Heb 9:12). He "offered *himself* without spot to God" (Heb 9:14). When he "entered in *once* into the holy place, having obtained eternal redemption for us" (Heb 9:12), the repetitive offerings of "bulls and goats, and the ashes of an heifer sprinkling the unclean" (Heb 9:13) had come to an end. For "Christ was *once* offered to bear the sins of many" (Heb 9:28). And when, at his death, "the veil of the temple was rent in twain from the top to the bottom" (Matt 27:51), the way was opened for us to enter directly to the most holy presence of God the Father (Eph 2:18). No longer was the mediation of an earthly priest necessary. For in Christ, the "one mediator" (1 Tim 2:5), we come to God; for Christ our mediator is himself God.

The benefits of Christ's offering himself as the atonement for sin accrue to those who were the subjects of the Covenant of Grace, those whom God the Father had given to him to redeem. But before we look directly at the benefits that thus accrue to them, it is necessary to remark briefly on the respects in which significance and satisfaction in Christ's atonement have reference to God himself and to Christ in his eternal Person. For at this point we are aware of the fulfillment of the prophecy of Isaiah: "He shall see of the travail of his soul, and shall be satisfied" (Isa 53:11). The travail of his soul, the results of the redemptive work that Christ came to do, are those for whom he gave his life, and now, at the right hand of the Father, he looks on them with satisfaction and divine complacence. Should it not be a comfort, encouragement, and joy to every struggling

---

28. Calvin, *Institutes*, 494–502.
29. Westminster Shorter Catechism, Question 25.

redeemed soul in this world, to know that their divine redeemer is at this time looking with satisfaction and pleasure on them, taking his own joy in them as he continually intercedes for them to the Father?

But we should be delinquent at this crucial point if we did not recall the benefit of reward that Christ obtained for himself for, and at the end of, his faithful completion of the work in this world that the Father had given him to do. For now he has been honored in that he has "sat down on the right hand of the Majesty on high" (Heb 1:3), made "heir of all things" (Heb 1:2), and "by inheritance obtained a more excellent name" than that of the angels (Heb 1:4). For because he "became obedient unto death, even the death of the cross . . . God also hath highly exalted him, and given him a name which is above every name: that at the name of Jesus every knee should bow" (Phil 2:8–10). The first Adam failed, as we have seen, to keep and honor the law of God and to sustain his obligations under the covenant in which he was established. Had he not failed he would have merited eternal life. But now the second Adam has fulfilled all the covenantal requirements. He has satisfied all the demands of the law for us, and he has paid to the full the penalty that had accrued to us for our having broken the law. Having done so, "when he had by himself purged our sins" (Heb 1:3), he was rewarded with the glory that the Father had reserved for him.

Finally in that connection, we may observe the respect in which God the Father himself is glorified in the completed redemptive work of his Son. For the end and objective of all that God had decreed in the Covenant of Redemption was that he himself should be glorified in the glory which it was his intention and design to bestow on his Son. On the night on which he was betrayed, at the end of the supper and before he went to the Garden of Gethsemane, Christ said to his eleven disciples (Judas having by then departed to consummate his perfidious plot), "now is the Son of man glorified, and God is glorified in him. If God be glorified in him, God shall also glorify him in himself, and shall straightway glorify him" (John 13:31–32). The cross points to the divine satisfaction of the Persons of the Godhead in the completion of what had been purposed in the eternal Covenant of Redemption. And God is glorified in the fact that his attributes of longsuffering, love, grace, mercy, wisdom, truth, and covenantal faithfulness are displayed to the heavenly hosts and to all his rational creation.

But what do we intend when we speak of the glory of God? It was displayed throughout the universe, we have seen, by the atonement of Christ. But there is what we may call a manward aspect of the demonstration of God's glory, a manward aspect that comes to expression only because the benefits of the death of Christ are reflected in the lives of his people. The imperative that rests on those people is that all things are to be done to the glory of God (1 Cor 10:31). We may say, then, that the glory of God exists in the demonstration to all his rational creation, in the heavenly realm and on the earth, of his infinite perfections. In fact, when we as his people are called on to do all things to the glory of God, the honor thereby placed upon us is that we are privileged to participate in precisely what has been said, namely the demonstration of the infinite perfections of God. That is the final reason why we are called upon to be like Christ our Savior. And though the reflection of his perfections in us as we live out our days in this vale of tears may be faltering and indistinct, the assurance that steels our spirits and lightens our way is the knowledge that "when he shall appear, we shall be like him" (1 John 3:2).

God the Father is glorified in the work of his Son, firstly in that the complete objectives of his covenantal decrees have been realized; and secondly, in the fact that thereby his glorious attributes are displayed. But overarching, in a sense, the eternal attributes of God thus displayed, is the demonstration of the fact that God is a God of love. "God so *loved* the world" (John 3:16). "God commendeth his *love* toward us, in that, while we were yet sinners, Christ died for us" (Rom 5:8). "He hath chosen us in [Christ] before the foundation of the world . . . in *love*: Having predestinated us unto the adoption of children by Jesus Christ to himself" (Eph 1:4–5). And "herein is love, not that we loved God, but that *he loved us*, and sent his Son to be the propitiation for our sins" (1 John 4:10). The love of God for his people is a sovereign, unchangeable, and perfect love. It is the same, "yesterday, and today, and for ever" (Heb 13:8). God declared to the prophet Malachi: "I am the LORD, I change not," (Mal 4:6). God does not love his people because Christ died for them, to reconcile them to himself. The contrary is true. Christ died for the people of God because God loved them. In the demonstration of that love God has declared to all of the hosts of heaven and all humanity that he is not only a covenant-making God, but a covenant-keeping God. The cross of Christ displays the glory of God in that it declares the wisdom of God. For the angels, we are told, are occupied in peering over the rim of heaven to observe the work of Christ and the church that follows him, in their attempt to understand something of what God in his unimaginable wisdom has done. These are things "the angels desire to look into" (1 Pet 1:12).

Our meditations are directed also to the benefits that accrue from the cross of Christ to those he thereby redeemed. It is the committed and undertaken redemptive office of the Holy Spirit to apply to those for whom Christ died the gifts and benefits he purchased for them. Those gifts include, notably, the gifts of repentance and faith whereby we come to him for rescue and relief. The Spirit accomplishes that communication of benefits "by working faith in us, and thereby uniting us to Christ in our effectual calling."[30] More extensively, there are conveyed to us by that means the benefits of justification, adoption, and sanctification. The recognition of those benefits opens to view a magnificent terrain of life in Christ, the detailed exposition of which cannot detain us at this point. We shall return to them in the following chapter. But it can be said that all that the believer in Christ enjoys accrues to him because, by virtue of the applicatory work of the Holy Spirit in regeneration and in the process of sanctification, he is joined to Christ in an organic, vital, spiritual, and indissoluble union.[31]

The Catechism we have referred to at several places continues its exploration of the benefits that accrue from Christ's work on the cross to observe that "the benefits which in this life do accompany or flow from justification, adoption, and sanctification, are: assurance of God's love, peace of conscience, joy in the Holy Ghost, increase of grace, and perseverance therein to the end."[32] It is worthy of emphasis that, as has just been said, the fact of the believer's union with Christ guarantees his eternal destiny and security. The scriptural data are copious. Those whom Christ redeemed have by reason of their existential union with him been "raised up together, and made to sit together in heavenly places in Christ Jesus" (Eph 2:6). They are "risen with Christ" (Col 3:1). The Christian, it follows, is a person of two existences and two outlooks. He exists now as a citizen of heaven and he is a citizen of this world. That being so, his entire outlook is determined by his citizenship of heaven, at the same time as he is left, in the very nature of the case, to command

---

30. Westminster Shorter Catechism, Question 30.

31. The related doctrines of adoption and union with Christ are explored more expansively in Vickers, *When God Converts a Sinner*, 114–44.

32. Westminster Shorter Catechism, Question 36.

an outlook on things in this world that is influenced by his identity as a servant of Christ.

The benefits of redemption by the cross include, most notably, the fact that now, at the right hand of the Father, Christ continually makes intercession for his people as they wait in this world for his coming again to receive them to himself. The Christian believer is the beneficiary of all that is involved on his behalf in the heavenly high priestly office of Christ. Two things are to be said in that connection. First, the heavenly high priestly office and function of our Lord involve the twofold benefits of first, intercession, and secondly, sympathy. Christ's heavenly concern for the care of those whom he is bringing to glory is without shadow or variation. It will be consummated at the last day in the resurrection of the saints and their eternal reign with him. That intercessory care extends to the point of carrying their prayers to the Father. Christ hears and receives the Christian's prayer, he knows even the unexpressed and inexpressible groanings of the Christian heart, and he interprets them to the Father. That is an aspect of what we observed at an earlier point as the satisfaction that our Lord in heaven takes in those he redeemed, the "travail of his soul."

Second, we observe that, as was said at the beginning, Christ, the divine Son of God in divine personhood, died for his people in his human nature. He rose in that same human nature. He ascended to heaven in that human nature, and it is now, in his full personhood, in the same human nature joined in union with his divine nature, that he conducts his heavenly high priestly office on our behalf. The fact that our Lord's human nature is involved in his heavenly priestly office and function guarantees the promise of his word: "We have not an high priest which cannot be touched with the feeling of our infirmities; but was in all points tempted like as we are, yet without sin. Let us therefore come boldly to the throne of grace, that we may obtain mercy, and find grace to help in time of need" (Heb 4:15–16). Our Lord himself has tasted the temptations and sorrows to which we are subject. He knows our frame. He knows all about us and all that can befall us in this short uncertain life and earthly pilgrimage. He knows the human soul because he, too, is human, and he has experienced all that we can encounter on the level of emotion and joy or distress. His human nature, the knowledge and awareness of human existence that human nature involves, informs his divine personhood as he acts on our behalf and as our intercessor in all of our relations with God.

Finally, it is apposite to the meaning of the cross to observe that certain benefits accrue from the work of Christ on the cross to those who do not, and who never will, believe in him to the saving of their souls. The meaning of that can be put briefly.

The objective of Christ's going to the cross was to save a people for himself in anticipation of the eternal kingdom they will share with him. It was his objective to establish and preserve his church in this world and then in due time to welcome his church triumphant to himself. We can properly say that all of God's actions, all of his providential, immanent interventions in the course of the history of the world, are eventuated in the interest of his church. But the ages of history must continue to run until all those whom Christ redeemed, including those not yet born, are brought to him and to the realization of sins forgiven. All that is therefore necessary must be done by the sovereign grace of God as he looks upon the unfolding history of the world. That means, in short, that it is by God's *common grace* that the world is preserved, its culture is developed, and all of its personal histories are eventuated.

A final reality must therefore be noted. That is that *common grace is to be understood as a part of Christology*. I have put the issue in those terms in order to emphasize the fact that the administration of God's common grace is what it is in order to permit and effect the full realization of the fruits of what Christ accomplished in his substitutionary dying on the cross. God's common grace is effective in the world because Christ by his atonement has saved a church that is being progressively called out of the world.

May he give us grace to live out the days he entrusts to us to the glory of God who has saved us at no less a price than the gift and the death of his own Son, to whom be glory for ever.

4

Justification and the Christian Life

THE DIVINE INTENTIONS OF the Covenant of Grace led uninterruptedly to the cross of Christ. The death of Christ on the cross, tragic as it was, was not a catastrophe for which no reason existed or was to be found. It was not merely a random episode, a blip on the course of history that could, when it occurred, be shunted aside as the lives of men and nations moved on. On the cross of Christ, the Son of God, with a deliberateness born of divine counsel, died in the place of sinners. The apostle Peter on the Day of Pentecost stated to the "men of Israel" that they had "by wicked hands crucified and slain" one who was "delivered by the determinate counsel and foreknowledge of God" (Acts 2:22–23).

It was true, lamentably true, that the people on that day did not know what they were doing. For as the apostle Paul was later to say, "none of the princes of this world," not Caiaphas or Pontius Pilate or the leaders of Israel, or, for that matter, the common people, had sufficient understanding to know that they were crucifying the Lord of glory. For as Paul said, "had they known it [had they known that it was the long-promised Messiah they were crucifying], they would not have crucified the Lord of glory" (1 Cor 2:8). The death of Christ was, on the level of its actual occurrence, an act of ignorance. But the ignorance, though it was sincere, was culpable. Christ had come "unto his own, and his own received him not" (John 1:11), because their eyes were blinded and they could not see.

That the death of Christ occurred in accordance with divine counsel, that it fulfilled the terms of the Covenant of Grace, is stated quite clearly in the seventeenth-century confessions of faith that systematized the Reformed theology. Those confessions strike to the heart of what is now before us as encapsulating the significance of the cross of Christ. That is that by repentance, faith, and trust in Christ the believing sinner is justified from his sin and enters into a new life in union with Christ. The Westminster Confession of Faith (1647), The Savoy Declaration of Faith (1658), and The Second London (Baptist) Confession (1689) each state that the acts of saving faith that lead to justification are "by virtue of the covenant of grace."[1] That confessional linkage of justification to God's salvific covenant challenges our understanding of the principal acts and aspects of the Christian life. It first states "the principal acts of saving faith." They are threefold: "accepting, receiving, and resting upon Christ alone." Then there is stated the threefold results to which those actions lead: "justification, sanctification, and eternal life."

The Confessions at that point are saying two things. First, those acts of saving faith ("accepting, receiving, and resting upon Christ") do themselves have efficacy for the objectives they realize ("justification, sanctification, and eternal life") only by reason of the benefits accruing from "the covenant of grace." Secondly, it follows that both the acts themselves and the objectives they realize are what they are because they were foreordained in the divine formulation of the Covenant of Grace. We state that second conclusion in other terms. It is not only that the Covenant of Grace contemplated the *ends* and *objectives* that have been stated. But the very *means*, the acts themselves that conduce to those ends, have been foreordained as elements of the Covenant of Grace. Every instance of individual saving faith is itself foreordained as an integral aspect of that covenant. What that is saying is that salvation in all its parts is by the grace of God. It destroys every suggestion that salvation is an autosoterism on an individual's part or that his salvation is due to his own action or merit, on the one hand, or a divine-human synergism on the other. It insists, to the contrary, that salvation is a divine monergism.

If, then, our doctrines of salvation and the Christian life are to be biblically-consistent they must also find their grounding in the biblical doctrine of the covenant. It is for that reason that Reformed theology has been properly described as covenant theology. The reality and the meaning of God's covenantal purpose provide the fundamental hermeneutical principle in terms of which we hear the Scriptures speak. By that we mean that when we marshal our understanding of the acts of salvation under the heading of the *ordo salutis* (the order of application

---

1. Westminster Confession of Faith, XIV:2, and similar in the Savoy Declaration and the Baptist Confession.

of the benefits of Christ's redemption), each of those acts is to be seen as covenantally grounded and warranted. In the present instance of saving faith and justification, God's declarative-forensic statement of justification is what it is, it conveys its peculiar significance to those who are the beneficiaries of it, and it sustains its relation to all of the saving acts of God because its occurrence and import are vital aspects of the administration of God's Covenant of Grace. We speak, therefore, of covenantal justification.

The cry of Job is the cry of the human heart that rings down the corridors of time: "How should man be just with God?" (Job 9:2). One is "just" with God when his relation to the law of God is what it ought to be. No one in his natural state since Adam's fall could lay claim to that condition. There is none righteous. Not one. "For all have sinned, and come short of the glory of God" (Rom 3:23). "The scripture [that is, what has been truthfully and extensively declared by the Scriptures] hath concluded all under sin" (Gal 3:22). How, then, could one attain to a relationship of justness, or righteousness, in relation to God who is the judge of all? There was no possibility that that could be realized by the existing human condition unless God himself should reestablish that "just" relationship by sending another just or righteous One to stand in the place of sinners. That he did, by sending his own eternal Son.

JUSTIFICATION

What, then, is justification? "Justification is an act of God's free grace, wherein he pardoneth all our sins, and accepteth us as righteous in his sight, only for the righteousness of Christ, imputed to us, and received by faith alone."[2] It is by the grace of God that one is justified. We have referred to the fact that salvation is a divine monergism because it is grounded in the divinely-appointed, substitutionary suffering, obedience, sacrifice, resurrection, and heavenly session of Christ. That monergism is further, and precisely, exhibited in the fact that the individual's saving faith is in turn the sovereign and unsolicited endowment of the Spirit of God to the human soul. When the faculties of the soul are renewed by that sovereign, secret, and unsolicited act of God in his conveying to the soul the grace of regeneration, the mind now sees and understands what was always there to be seen but was darkened by the

---

2. Westminster Shorter Catechism, Question 33.

enslavement of the mind to the god of this world (2 Cor. 4:4). The assent of the mind is therefore given with a new readiness to the explanation that God has made regarding the human condition. The cross of Christ is now seen in a light that before was inconceivable. The affective faculty of the soul is now turned from a hatred of God (Rom 1:30) to love God and seek after him. The soul that was averse from God now sees the law of God in a new context of righteousness and obligation. It now seeks a new and righteous alignment with the law of God, doing so with a new volition that is at last free from enslavement to sin. "Thy people," the Psalmist says in anticipation of that liberating work of God in the soul, "shall be willing in the day of thy power" (Ps 110:3). That is the result of the new perspective on the cross of Christ, the new vision of the "why" of the cross, that the new life in the soul has brought to the surface of consciousness. Now the individual who has been the beneficiary of the grace of regeneration turns to Christ in saving faith. John Murray has made the point when he said that "regeneration pushes itself into consciousness and expresses itself in the exercise of faith and repentance."[3]

In that manner, we see the cross of Christ as the culmination of God's ordering of the objectives of the Covenant of Grace. We say, therefore, that the suffering of Christ is to be understood as a covenantal suffering, as his incarnation was a covenantal incarnation, his obedience and death a covenantal obedience and death, and all of the aspects of his salvific accomplishment are in the same manner covenantally qualified. The monergistic circle that establishes and guarantees salvation is closed, accordingly, in the reality that saving faith is itself to be understood as covenantal faith. That is to say, all aspects of salvation occur within, and they discover their full meaning under the rubric of, the Covenant of Grace. For that reason we conclude that what we have been accustomed to refer to in our doctrinal formulation as the elements of the *ordo salutis*, as well as the acts of God that are elements of the accomplishment of redemption, are to be understood as covenantally qualified in the sense we have stated.

But within the tradition of Reformed-evangelical doctrine, widening interpretations on those levels exist and have troubled the church. In modern times, varying suggestions have emerged for the formation of new interpretive theological paradigms. Some have suggested that justification is by "obedient faith," where the introduction of the adjec-

3. Murray, *Collected Writings*, vol. 2, 198.

tive causes a slippage from the divine monergism of redemption to a divine-human synergism. For it is effectively proposed in that scheme of things that the human work of obedience is cooperative with faith in justification. In that case justification is by faith *and* works, and the repeated apostolic declaration that justification is by faith alone, is refuted and set aside.[4]

But the biblical data are clear. "A man is justified by faith without the deeds of the law" (Rom 3:28). "A man is not justified by the works of the law, but by faith of [or in] Jesus Christ ... for by the works of the law shall no flesh be justified" (Gal 2:16). The biblical doctrine, holding clearly to what has already been seen as the terms of the Covenant of Grace, requires it to be said that the *efficient cause* of salvation is the grace of God; the *meritorious cause* is the death of Christ; and the *instrumental cause* is the faith of the repentant sinner. On the basis of faith in Christ, justification is a once-for-all declarative, forensic statement of God that one is accounted righteous in God's sight on the grounds of the imputation to him of the forensic righteousness of Christ. The word "forensic" means "in relation to law." God's statement of justification is stated to be "forensic" because it declares the sinner to be "just" in the sense previously indicated; namely, that his relation to the law of God is now, because the righteousness of Christ has been placed to his account, reckoned to be what it ought to be.

Some theologians have argued, however, that notwithstanding any statement of God to the sinner in such terms at the point in time of repentance and faith, justification is not effected once-and-for-all at that time. It is said that a final statement of forensic justification awaits the day of judgment. Such a doctrinal construction again violates the clear meaning of the scriptural data. Given what we have seen as the once-for-allness of God's forensic declarative statements to the repentant sinner, the individual person enters thereby into a *state* of justification that cannot be reversed or stands in any need of supplementation. In the day of glory that individual will be more sanctified, but not more justified. That is because, as has been said, at regeneration the individual is joined to Christ.

It is necessary to be clear, on the basis of what has been said, that God's statement of justification is properly said to be "forensic" because

---

4. See, for example, the work of Shepherd, recently summarized in his *The Call of Grace*.

it has to do precisely and completely with the standing of a sinner in relation to the law of God. At that point, God looks on the repentant sinner as one whose relation to the law is not what it ought to be, and he observes the sinner to be therefore "ungodly" (Rom 5:6). But in order to remedy that condition God gives to the sinner the forensic righteousness of Christ. We have already encapsulated that fact by observing the reciprocal imputation that is involved. God places the guilt of the sinner's sin to Christ's account, and he places to the sinner's account the righteousness of Christ. Involved in justification, then, is an exchange that is totally and completely a matter of the reversal of a condition in relation to the law of God. The sinner who, at the point of faith is ungodly is, by virtue of the exchange, reckoned now to be godly.

In that respect, a further aspect of the divine action in justification should be observed. It is clearly stated in the Scriptures that "Christ died for the ungodly" (Rom 5:6), and that in doing so he bore the penalty of the guilt of those for whom he died (2 Cor 5:21). But the question arises: How could God the Father, in all justice, and remaining true to his eternal righteousness, punish in Christ the sins of others when the penalty must be borne only by those who were guilty. God who is himself truthful and eternally righteous could not lay the punishment for sin on his Son unless his Son was actually guilty. What, then, was to be done? In order to be able truthfully to *declare* his Son guilty and therefore liable to punishment, and for God to remain true to his own righteousness, it was necessary that God should first *constitute* his Son guilty. That is precisely what was done. God *constituted* Christ guilty by imputing to him the guilt of those for whom he was about to die. Christ was not constituted a sinner. He was constituted guilty of sin, not of any sin of his own, for he was sinless, but guilty by transference to him of the sin of the people for whom he died. Because he had been constituted guilty, God could rightly and justly lay the punishment of sin on him. By the same token, God could not truthfully *declare* any persons to be righteous who were not, in fact, righteous. The truthfulness of God again intervened in the transaction. In order, therefore, to be able truthfully to *declare* certain individuals righteous, it was necessary that God should first *constitute* them as righteous. Again, that is precisely what was done. God *constituted* those people righteous by imputing to them the forensic righteousness of Christ. By that reciprocal transaction the justice of God remained unimpaired. God was therefore "just, and the justifier of him which believeth in Jesus" (Rom 3:26).

On this highly important matter of constitutive righteousness, Murray has written insightfully: "Justification is both a declarative and a constitutive act of God's free grace. It is constitutive in order that it may be truly declarative. God must constitute the new relationship as well as declare it to be. The constitutive act consists in the imputation to us of the obedience and righteousness of Christ."[5] Acknowledging that the truthfulness and righteousness of God are involved at that point, Turretin has stated in that connection: "God cannot show favor to, nor justify anyone without a perfect righteousness. For since the judgment of God is according to truth, he cannot pronounce anyone just who is not really just. . . . By the righteousness and obedience of one, Christ, we are constituted righteous. . . . Justification takes place on account of the suretyship of Christ and the payment made for us by him."[6]

When the purely forensic nature and meaning of justification are thus exposed, it is to be observed that God's action of justification does not make a person holy. Holiness is not involved at that point. But if it is not justification that makes a person holy, what does? The answer turns on the reality and meaning of God's conveyance to the sinner of the sovereign grace of regeneration. It is by regeneration that one is made holy, and that grace having done its work in the soul of an individual, he turns to Christ in saving faith in the manner we have seen. There is then an important sense in which holiness is prior to justification. By that we mean that a person is holy in the sense in which, having been the beneficiary of a new creating work of the Holy Spirit, he is set apart for God in a completely new relationship. By the secret work of the Spirit of God in regeneration, a being "born again," as Christ referred to it in his nocturnal conversation with Nicodemus (John 3:3), a sinner is thereby "delivered from the power of darkness, and translated into the kingdom of [God's] dear Son" (See Col 1:13). That work of regeneration constitutes the individual as holy, not only in the positional sense that he is now set apart for God, but in the sense also that the Holy Spirit's work of sanctification in the life of the individual has thereby begun. That is because the faculties of soul have been endowed with new abilities and capacities in the manner we have seen, and a new *habitus* or disposition or principle

---

5. See Murray, *Redemption*, 154. See also Murray, *Romans*, vol. 1, 203–206.
6. Turretin, *Institutes*, vol. 2, 647, 651, 653.

of action has been divinely implanted in the soul. By regeneration one is made holy and his sanctification has begun; and by justification his status in relation to the law of God is radically changed to what it ought to be. In holiness and righteousness, then, the newborn person freely sets out on a life that is pleasing to God. Now and henceforth the Holy Spirit will so work in the life of the individual as to further his growth in holiness, or, as we shall see, his progressive sanctification.

SANCTIFICATION

In our initial comment on the statement of the seventeenth-century confessions we drew attention, first, to what they refer to as "the principal acts of saving faith." Secondly, we noted that those threefold acts, "accepting, receiving, and resting upon Christ," were instrumental to the realization of the threefold benefits of "justification, sanctification, and eternal life." A close covenantal relation exists between the respective trilogies of the *means* and the *ends* that were contemplated. The very acts that conduce to the objectives of justification, sanctification, and eternal life, the *means* as well as the *objectives* and *ends*, have been ordained as integral to the divine formation of the Covenant of Grace. That is what we mean by saying that all of the parts and aspects of our redemption and entrance to eternal life are what they are because of the grace of God. The cross of Christ, in the ways we have seen, projects its benefits to the Christian life. Let us now look at some further aspects of what is involved in that respect.

First, with recognition again of the pervasive implications of the fact that God's relations with his people are covenantal relations, God's covenantal lordship comes to effect in that he "works all things according to the counsel of his own will" (See Eph. 1:11). We are interested now in the "all things" that are at issue in that covenantal statement. If, as we have said, God in that divine working is sovereign in and over all of the affairs of men, does that sovereignty extend, we may ask, to *all* of the *actions* of men? We answer in the affirmative. Further, does that sovereignty extend to all of the *thoughts* of men? We again answer in the affirmative. And in that answer, as we shall see, we are anticipating a highly significant aspect of the work of the Holy Spirit in the process of the Christian believer's sanctification. In other words, the all-comprehending sovereignty of God requires it to be said that it is not possible for any individual to *do* anything that God has not ordained. It is not possible for man to *do* anything that God has not already thought. But further, our claim is that it is not possible for any individual to *think* anything that God has not already thought. "I know the things that come into your mind," God has said, "every one of them" (Ezek 11:5). He knows the thought because he ordained the thought. "The lot is cast into the lap; but the whole disposing thereof is of the LORD" (Prov 16:33). More particularly, "the king's heart is in the hand of the LORD, as the rivers of water; he turneth it whithersoever he will" (Prov 21:1).

The meaning of what is involved might be startling on its surface and it no doubt challenges in our thought the question of individual personal freedom or, as it most forcibly comes to expression, the freedom of the human will. We shall return to the point. But it would be grossly inadequate to say that the Spirit of God orders only the *external* events and experiences in the life of the individual he is committed to bring to glory. The Spirit moves in the *innermost recesses of the soul*. He thinks the thoughts of holiness in us, and he thereby structures our lives and our progress. What else would be the meaning and import of the apostle's exclamation to the Galatians, "I live; yet not I, but Christ liveth in me" (Gal 2:20)? The hymn writer, Harriet Auber, has captured the meaning of what is involved in the hymn that begins, "Our blest Redeemer, ere He breathed / His tender, last farewell, / A guide, a comforter, bequeathed / With us to dwell." And in the penultimate stanza the hymn writer reflects on the ministry of that Comforter to the soul and states significantly that "every thought of holiness [is] his alone."[7]

Secondly, we acknowledge that there is mystery involved in the sovereign work of the Spirit of God in the soul of man. That mystery exists within the orbit of the working of the Spirit at the same time as the individual person himself works out his salvation. "Work out your own salvation with fear and trembling," Paul said to the Philippians, "for it is God which worketh in you both to will and to do of his good pleasure" (Phil 2:12–13). The statement is not to the effect that the person can by his own individual working establish salvation for himself. If that were imagined to be the case, our doctrine would fall back into the autosoterism we have already rejected in favor of a divine monergism. Man would then be the effective source of his own salvation. Nor does the Philippian text state simply that God by his grace gives to his people the ability and power to live in obedience to his law. For the law of God remains the

---

7. Auber, *Our blest Redeemer, ere He breathed His tender, last farewell*, 209.

rule of life for God's people. That God does give grace to his people to that effect is, of course, true. But the text is saying, beyond that, that God does in fact accomplish in the lives of his people what he has ordained as the parts and progress of their conformation in holiness to the image of his Son. The Spirit is sovereign in sanctification. He accomplishes in and for his people what he has willed to do. In that sovereignty he is working sanctification in them by communicating to them the communicable attributes of God to the extent that, and in the degree that, he is preparing them for the place he has ordained they will occupy in the eternal kingdom of glory.

When the apostle states that God works in the Christian person "to will and to do of his good pleasure," a further and deeper divine prospect and objective come into view. The burden of the text should not be restricted to a manward aspect of what is involved, in the sense that concentration is confined to the benefits that accrue to the individual Christian in his own right. It is true that what the text contemplates is to be understood as contributing to the individual person's sanctification in the manner we have said. But in all of the divine working in and with his people, God's larger covenantal purposes and objectives must be held in view. Involved in the Philippians statement, then, is that God has bestowed on the Christian believer, and that he continues by his sanctifying grace to bestow on his people, the high privilege of their being, under God, the means of furthering the realization of what God has purposed to do "of his good pleasure."

That is so in the sense, again, that it reflects what we said previously regarding God's purpose that all things should be done to his glory and should reflect his glory. Our observation in that earlier context was to the effect that God's glory consisted in the demonstration to all his rational creatures, in heaven and in earth, of his infinite perfections. And when the Christian is enjoined to do all things to the glory of God (1 Cor 10:31), he is given the high privilege of being the reflection of that glory, in being the vehicle in whatever way God ordains of participating in and contributing to that high objective. So it is in the present case of the Christian believer's progress in sanctification. God works in the lives of his people in such a way that a twofold objective will be realized. First, by his working in them he gives them the motivation and encouragement to persevere in their part in the process of their sanctification. And second, by doing so he is using his sanctified people to further his objective of demonstrating his own glory. That is the high privilege of the Christian life.

"Sanctification," the catechism states, "is the work of God's free grace, whereby we are renewed in the whole man after the image of God, and are enabled more and more to die unto sin, and live unto righteousness."[8] We note that in the case of justification it was stated that it involved an *act* of God's free grace. Now in the case of sanctification it is stated that we are contemplating not an *act*, but a *work* of God's free grace. The difference is vitally important. In the case of justification, as we have seen, the sinner brings, and can bring, no work or merit of his own when, at the cross of Christ, he bows in repentance, faith, and trust before his sovereign redeemer. We have seen that faith is communicated to the soul by the grace of God in his sovereign conveyance to the sinner of the grace of regeneration. Saving faith is the "gift of God" (Eph 2:8). The sinner necessarily brings nothing of his own merit or works to the cross of Christ. Our Lord put it once and for all when he said that "no man can come unto me, except the Father which hath sent me draw him" (John 6:44). And in the same context Christ therefore stated that "all that the Father giveth me shall come to me; and him that cometh to me I will in no wise cast out" (John 6:37). In that development of God's purpose in the calling and salvation of sinners we have the fulfillment of the prophecy of Jeremiah of old: "I have loved thee with an everlasting love: therefore with lovingkindness have I drawn thee" (Jer 31:3). Justification is a once-for-all sovereign, declarative, forensic statement of God.

But now that the justified individual is established in the new standing with God that we have seen justification to imply, now that he is no longer "dead in trespasses and sins" (Eph 2:1) but now has new and eternal life in the soul, he is able to do what was never possible or of any interest to him before. He is now able, by the supporting grace of God, to "work out his salvation." That is to say, he is now able to understand what it is God requires of him that he might live to the glory of God, he now loves the law of God, and he is now able to work out in his life a new path of obedience to that law. That is why the apostle said to the Philippian Christians, "work out your salvation." They were to work it out, to work out the meaning of it, and to discover all the ways in which the new life is to be lived in such a manner as to be pleasing before God. The apostle

---

8. Westminster Shorter Catechism, Question 35.

Peter struck the same theme when he said: "Give diligence to make your calling and election sure" (2 Pet 1:10). It was in no sense true that the Christians to whom Peter wrote could or should do anything to establish their election. That was due to the sovereign will and grace of God. What Peter is saying is that the Christian must work out the meaning of his salvation in such a way as to make his election sure to himself.

But at the same time as all that is true, the believer's progress in sanctification, his progressive conformance to the likeness of Christ, is what is now stated to be the *work* of God's free grace by the Holy Spirit. The *act* of God was done in his declaration of justification. Now the *work* of God continues in conjunction with the believer's own working as his sanctification progresses and develops. The work of the Holy Spirit in preparing the saints of God for their place in glory is analogous to what was involved in the preparation for the temple that Solomon built. "The house, when it was in building, was built of stone made ready before it was brought thither: so that there was neither hammer nor axe nor any tool of iron heard in the house, while it was in building" (1 Kgs 6:7). So now, the Holy Spirit is at work in this life preparing his people for their place in heaven. For at the point of entrance to heaven the preparation will have been completed. There will be no further sanctification in heaven. The preparatory process of sanctification will have come to an end, and all will be ready for the glorious eternal temple of God. In the process to that end, the Spirit so supervises, orders, directs, and guides the operation of personal free wills that all that he has purposed does in fact eventuate.

The sovereignty of God in sanctification is well displayed in the apostolic summary: "Of him [of, or by, God] are ye in Christ Jesus, who of God [or by God] is made unto us wisdom, and righteousness, and *sanctification*, and redemption" (1 Cor 1:30, italics added). Christ is our sanctification. We have said that in the predeterminate council of the Godhead the redemptive office of the Holy Spirit was that of applying to those for whom Christ died the benefits of his redemption. Now when the Corinthian text states that Christ is made sanctification to us, the respect in which that is so is twofold. First, Christ is our sanctification in that by his substitutionary life and death he established the ground of our sanctification. Second, he is our sanctification in that he ministers to us by his Spirit. We recall his words to his disciples in his supper discourses on the night on which he was betrayed. "I will send [the Comforter] unto you. . . . when he, the Spirit of truth, is come . . . he shall not speak of himself; but whatsoever he shall hear, that shall he speak. . . . He shall glorify me: for he shall receive of mine, and shall show it unto you" (John 16:7, 13-14). Christ is our sanctification by the ministry to us of his Spirit.

THE IMPERATIVES OF FAITH

If, then, the cross of Christ has for the believer whom Christ draws to himself the benefits we have observed, the question to be faced is that of what, in fact, is the work in sanctification that is required of the believer? At that point the directions of the Scriptures are copious. The imperative is placed before us in various ways. "As ye have therefore received Christ Jesus the Lord," Paul says to the Colossians, "so walk ye in him" (Col 2:6). Later in the same letter Paul places the challenge of Christian living before the Colossians in a way that brings together the high doctrines that are explanatory of their position on the one hand, and the imperatives that must be seen to follow from it on the other. "If [or because] ye then be risen with Christ, seek those things which are above" (Col 3:1). The apostle has stated there, first, the high doctrine that by reason of their belief in Christ and their union with him, they have been "risen with Christ." That is the doctrine and fact from which Paul could not escape and which informed the very center of his thought. He had said the same thing to the Ephesian Christians: "[God] hath raised us up together, and made us sit together in heavenly places in Christ Jesus" (Eph 2:6). But now in the Colossian text, Paul, having reminded the believers there of their same high status, immediately follows that by the imperative that it implies: "seek the things which are above."

In the same paragraph, the apostle continues the alternation between high doctrine and the practical application in the form of the imperatives that follow from it. "Christ," he says, "sitteth on the right hand of God." Therefore, "set your affections on things above, not on things on the earth." Then again, a point of high doctrine that is relevant to the Christian's situation follows: "For ye are dead, and your life is hid with Christ in God." (Col 3:1-3). And then follows the most direct instruction that is relevant to the whole matter of the Christian believer's sanctification. "Mortify therefore your members which are upon the earth; fornication, uncleanness . . . [and a sobering catalogue of sins follows] . . . In the which ye also walked some time, when ye lived in them. But now ye also put off all these" (Col 3:5-8). That, Paul says, is possible because the Christians have "put off the old man with his deeds; And have put on the new man, which is renewed in knowledge after the image of him that created him" (Col 3:9–10).

The part the believer plays in his sanctification is, substantially, his careful obedience to the law of God. He now loves the law, and in his pursuit of godliness he strains every nerve to live in obedience to it. In that, he seeks the aid of the Spirit of God. He cultivates the presence of God. But paramountly, it is the believer's responsibility to so conduct his life that the tendencies to sin within him are mortified, or put to death. "For if ye live after the flesh," the apostle stated to the Romans, "ye shall die: but if ye through the Spirit do mortify the deeds of the body, ye shall live" (Rom 8:13). The apostolic teaching amounts to the fact that there will be no progress in sanctification unless and until there is progress in the mortification of sin. Again, the apostle brings to convergence the responsibility of the believer and the empowering ministry to him of the Holy Spirit. It is "through the Spirit" that the errant deeds of the flesh are to be mortified.

But the question arises: What results if the Christian, in fact, does not conduct himself in such a way as to pursue holiness and likeness to Christ in the manner we have contemplated as now being obligatory? Does the possibility exist, in such a case, that the whole enterprise of redemption, sanctification, and preparation for heaven falls to the ground? The answer is "No." For Christ has said regarding those whom he draws to himself, the sheep for whom he died, that "I give unto them eternal life; and they shall never perish, neither shall any man pluck them out of my hand" (John 10:28). Those whom Christ has redeemed are definitively saved. They can never perish. We saw in an earlier context that for Adam, his created status implied for him *posse non peccare*, or possible not to fall. But he fell. For the Christian believer, on the other hand, that positional status is dramatically changed. Of the Christian it is to be said, *non posse peccare*, or not possible to fall. The difference should be noted carefully. What is meant is that the Christian believer cannot now fall from his newly-established status and be eternally lost. That is because in the process of effecting his salvation, God by his Holy Spirit has joined the believer in a vital and indissoluble union with Christ.

The apostle made precisely the same argument to the Romans. Consider his statement: "Where sin abounded, grace did much more abound" (Rom 5:20). The "sin abounded" refers to Adam's fall. We have looked at its incidence and the transmission of its effects. But Paul is here saying that grace more abounded in that salvation by the grace of God does not merely raise the renewed individual to the level or status that Adam occupied before he fell. Grace *more* abounded. It raises an individual to a higher level and state than Adam enjoyed. That higher state is, as has been said, that he has been joined to Christ. He cannot, therefore, fall from the position in which, by grace, he now stands.

But the question remains: What if the believer is delinquent in pursuing the holiness of life to which he is called? The answer was given by the writer of the letter to the Hebrews when he had to deal with precisely that question: "Whom the Lord loveth he chasteneth, and scourgeth every son whom he receiveth. . . . Now no chastening for the present seemeth to be joyous, but grievous: nevertheless afterward it yieldeth the peaceable fruit of righteousness unto them which are exercised thereby" (Heb 12:6, 11). In other words, God by his Spirit will not allow his redeemed people to remain delinquent in pursuing a life of sanctifying obedience to him. He will exercise his discipline in such a way as to keep his people on the upward path to glory. The Psalmist said the same thing. "Thy rod and thy staff they comfort me" (Ps 23:4). God uses the rod of discipline, as well as his staff of comfort for the eternal good of his people.

The Christian believer, by reason of the graces of regeneration and justification, is now a new person in Christ. That is well declared by the apostle in his statement that "if any man be in Christ, he is a new creature: old things are passed away; behold, all things are become new" (2 Cor 5:17). That newness of life is what it is because, in a remarkable act of imputation by God, when Christ died, the believer died. The apostle put it by saying that "our old man is crucified with him [Christ]" (Rom 6:6). By reason of one's participation in the death of Christ, the believer is not made sinless. The Christian sins, and the meaning of his sin needs carefully to be understood. What has to be said is that the Christian is now a new person, described by a new nature. The man is, we may say, what his nature is. He is one person, of one nature, and that a new nature, and it is part of the reality of his life that in that new nature he both glorifies God and, it has also to be said, he sins. The question follows: How should that be so?

Let us observe, first, that not all contemporary theologians have grasped adequately the relations involved in what has just been said. Some have maintained that in the regenerate Christian there remains both an old nature and a new nature. The old *man*, they say, is dead, on the basis of Romans 6:6. But, it is then said, the old *nature* is still very much alive. That misconception has been furthered by a translation of the Scriptures that consistently translates the word "flesh" as it refers to the Christian person as "sinful nature."[9] It has to be said, to the contrary, that while the Christian believer is one person with one new nature, there nevertheless remains within him the residue of an old principle of action that is capable of motivating his actions and giving rise to occasions of sin.

The nineteenth-century theologian, Robert Dabney, has addressed the doctrine at some length. He observes of the individual that he "has one consciousness, he knows that he is one indivisible personality."[10] And Dabney goes on to discuss what it is that regeneration in the individual involves. He comments that it "*reverses* the moral *habitus* [i.e. disposition or principle of action] of the believer's will, prevalently [that is, a new disposition is prevalent, or prevails, in the soul], but not at first absolutely, and . . . the work of progressive sanctification carries on the change, thus omnipotently begun, towards that absolute completeness which we must possess on entering heaven. In the carnal state, the *habitus* [or disposition] of the sinner's will is absolutely and exclusively godless. In the regenerate state it is prevalently but not completely godly. In the glorified state it is absolutely and exclusively godly."[11] But the important fact is that the Christian is "one indivisible personality," and it is that one person who, by virtue of his regeneration, is now disposed, but not yet absolutely, to reflect in his life and actions the perfect holiness of God. As Dabney correctly has it, "the Bible is still farther from saying that the renewed man has two '*natures*.'"[12]

Referring to those who hold the "two natures" theory, Dabney says: "We challenge them to produce a text from the New Testament where it is said that regeneration is the implantation of a 'new *nature*' beside the old; or that the renewed man has two hostile '*natures*,' or any such language. . . . Paul . . . teaches that the renewed man (one man and one

---

9. See the New International Version at Romans 8:5. The question of translation at that point and its relation to the doctrine of the new nature in the regenerate Christian has been addressed by Martin, *Accuracy of Translation*.

10. Dabney, *Discussions*, vol. 1, 196.

11. Ibid., 196–97.

12. Ibid., 194.

nature still) is imperfect, having two principles of volition mixed in the motives even of the same acts; but he does not teach that he has become 'two men,' or has 'two natures' in him. Paul's idea is, that man's one nature, originally wholly sinful, is by regeneration made imperfectly holy, but progressively so."[13] "[The doctrine of the two natures in man] contradicts the consciousness of every Christian, even the most unlearned; for just so surely as he has one consciousness, he knows he is one indivisible personality, and that he is one agent and has *only one will*, swayed indeed by mixed and diverse motives."[14]

It has been said by some that when one sins, it is the old nature that sins. That, however, overlooks that when one sins it is the *person* who sins, and it is the *person* who is alarmingly responsible for his sin. But why, then, does the Christian sin, and how is sin to be explained? A disposition to sin, Dabney has just said, remains in the Christian. The situation has been explained also by John Murray when he says that "the believer is a new man, a new creation, but he is a new man not yet made perfect. Sin dwells in him still, and he still commits sin. He is necessarily the subject of progressive renewal. . . . But this *progressive* renewal is not represented as the putting off of the old man and the putting on of the new, nor is it to be conceived of as the progressive crucifixion of the old man."[15] We are to say, then, that the Christian is a new person, characterized and described by a new nature, but that the faculties of his soul, while they have been renewed with new endowments in the manner we have seen, have not yet been made perfect. They are still capable of being deceived by sin, by old habits, by the allurements of the world, and by the subtleties of the devil and his angels. That ability to be led into sin by old habits and old imaginations remains by virtue of the still-existing principle of "indwelling sin." It is what Paul wrote about so eloquently in the seventh chapter of his letter to the Romans. Sin dwells within the Christian because, while his faculties have been renewed in principle, their transformation into the image of the holiness of God has not yet been perfected.

We can put that differently in the language of the seventeenth-century Puritan theologian, John Owen. In his treatise, *A Discourse Concerning the Holy Spirit*, Owen addresses the reality of sin in the life of

13. Ibid., 192–93.
14. Ibid., 196.
15. Murray, *Principles of Conduct*, 219.

the truly regenerate person. "In those who are thus constantly inclined and disposed unto all the acts of a heavenly, spiritual life, there are yet remaining contrary dispositions and inclinations also."[16] Here we see the same understanding of sin as is reflected in the argument of Dabney that we have just noted. Owen goes on to say that "there are yet in them [regenerate Christian individuals] inclinations and dispositions to sin, proceeding from the *remainders* of a contrary habitual principle."[17] What Owen refers to as the "contrary habitual principle" is again a reference to what is described in the Scriptures as indwelling sin. It is against that sinful principle, and with the objective of the destruction of it, that the Christian is directed to the duty of the mortification of sin (Rom 8:13).

ETERNAL LIFE

The confessional statement we adduced at the beginning states that the "principal acts of saving faith" are, by God's grace, directed to the objectives of "justification, sanctification, and eternal life." We now reflect briefly on the meaning of eternal life and consider its relation to what we have said of justification and sanctification.

A careful reading of the confession makes it clear that "eternal life" is to be seen as referring to the state in which the Christian believer is established as a result of what God had ordained as the Covenant of Grace. But eternal life, as the confession brings that into focus at this point, is not to be understood as a blessing that is *conditional upon*, in the sense that it *awaits*, justification and progressive sanctification. It is true that a full realization of the fact and the benefits of eternal life *follows experientially* those other blessings. But the entrance to eternal life is to be guarded as *prior* to justification. That is because the entrance to eternal life turns on the fact, and on the Holy Spirit's act, of an individual's regeneration by the sovereign grace of God. At regeneration the individual who is the beneficiary of that grace is baptized into the body of Christ (1 Cor 12:13), has the seal of God as belonging to him placed upon him, "sealed with that holy Spirit of promise" (Eph 1:13), and is joined to Christ in a vital and indissoluble union. The priority of that union has been well stated by Berkhof: "The initial act is that of Christ,

---

16. Owen, *Holy Spirit*, 488. See also the discussion in Ferguson, *John Owen on the Christian Life*, 64.

17. Owen, idem.

who unites believers to himself *by regenerating them* and thus producing faith in them. On the other hand, the believer also unites himself to Christ by a conscious act of faith, and continues the union, under the influence of the Holy Spirit, by the constant exercise of faith."[18]

Berkhof has stated concisely aspects of what we hold as the *ordo salutis*, or the order of application of redemption. He has emphasized the distinction between the *endowment* of faith on the one hand, or the endowment of the capacity to exercise faith, and the subsequent *exercise* of faith on the other. The *endowment* of faith is the *immediate* work of the Spirit of God that occurs at a point in time. The *exercise* of faith, or the activation of the newly endowed capacity of faith, occurs in time and may be characterized by any of several time dimensions. Murray observes in relation to those actions that "regeneration pushes itself into consciousness and expresses itself in the exercises of faith and repentance."[19] But as to regeneration itself and the implications of it, Murray refers to regeneration as that act "of which faith and repentance are the immediate effects in our consciousness."[20]

We distinguish, then, between the *ground* on which God's statement of justification can be made on the one hand, and the *act* of justification on the other. The *ground* of justification is the completed substitutionary work of Christ. The *act* of justification follows God's response in time to the individual's exercise of faith and trust in Christ. It is, of course, true that there are aspects of the believer's realization of his eternal state that necessarily follow justification and sanctification. For the reality of eternal life expands its meaning to the state that will exist and be experienced in the life that is to come. But what is at issue at this point is that when, and because, the conditions necessary to justification and sanctification have been met (the work of Christ has fulfilled the conditions specified in the Covenant of Grace and the regenerating grace of God has conveyed the gift of faith to the soul) then at that point and at that time the believer is an indefectible partaker of eternal life.

Justification and sanctification, then, both involve, in different respects, declarative statements of God. We have already noted the once-for-all forensic statement of God that amounts to the repentant sinner's justification. Against that declarative statement, the sinner enters into a

18. Berkhof, *Systematic Theology*, 450, italics added.
19. John Murray, *Collected Writings*, vol. 2, 198.
20. Ibid., 115.

new experiential state, the state of *being* justified. "Therefore being justified by faith, we have peace with God" (Rom 5:1). As to sanctification, we note the following. First, it is at the point of regeneration that the individual to whom that grace is communicated is thereby definitively and once-for-all transferred from the kingdom of Satan to the kingdom of God. At that point his transference from wrath to grace definitively occurs. God has thereby "delivered us from the power of darkness, and hath translated us into the kingdom of his dear Son" (Col 1:13). Then as there is a once-for-allness about God's statements of justification and adoption into his family, so there is a once-for-allness in the transference from the one kingdom to the other that regeneration involves and which constitutes eternal life. When the repentant sinner responds in faith to God's statement that he "gave his only begotten Son, that whosoever believeth in him should not perish, but have everlasting life" (John 3:16), eternal life has begun. At the moment of regeneration from which saving faith emanates, sanctification has begun. Because that is so, we agree with John Murray's statements regarding what he refers to at that point as "definitive sanctification."[21] The new state of holiness in which the beneficiary of grace now stands is what is referred to as the individual's definitive sanctification. He is now holy in the sight of God.

Beyond that divine statement of definitive sanctification, however, is the progressive work of the Spirit in the life of the believer that amounts to what we have observed as his *progressive* sanctification. The redemptive work of God comes to consummation in the life of the individual by his deliverance from the guilt, the power, and the pollution of sin. The deliverance from the *guilt* of sin we have inspected under the heading of the justifying act of God, in the reciprocal imputation of the sinner's guilt to Christ and the imputation of Christ's righteousness to the sinner. The *power* of sin, or what we have seen as the ability of the enemy of our souls to activate the principle of sin that remains within us, presses upon the individual throughout his life in this world. It is the office of the Holy Spirit to bring his divine influence to bear on the consciousness and life of the individual in such a way that the power of sin is progressively destroyed. The newborn person in Christ is progressively cleansed from the *pollution* of sin by the work of God in the soul that takes up what is

---

21. See Murray, "Definitive Sanctification" in *Collected Writings*, vol. 2, 277–84.

referred to as progressive sanctification, to which definitive sanctification is the necessary antecedent.[22]

INDIVIDUAL FREEDOM AND SANCTIFICATION

In our discussion of the work of the Spirit of God in the Christian believer's sanctification it was noted that God's ordination extends not only to the *actions* of the individual, but also to his *thoughts*. We took note of Harriet Auber's hymn that includes the arresting line, "every thought of holiness [is] his alone." What, then, is to be said of individual freedom?

We do not need to enter at this point the long and philosophic discussion of the freedom of the will. I have addressed that in other places.[23] The upshot of the question for our present purposes is that the individual will is not free in an isolated sense to determine its own action, but that it necessarily acts in conformity with the state, decisions, and motivations of the faculties of the soul. In Adam's prelapsarian state an undisturbed harmony existed among the faculties. The soul was then characterized by free will in the fullest sense. The Westminster Shorter Catechism makes the point. When our first parents were "left to the *freedom of their own will*" they "fell from the estate wherein they were created."[24] That initial state of free will existed because the mind, the intellectual faculty, naturally knew God and responded with clarity and uncluttered reason to the knowledge of God that was inherent in Adam's created condition. At the same time, with the affective or emotional faculty Adam naturally loved God, and the natural disposition, the *habitus* implicit in the soul, moved our first parent to love the law of God and to love the work of obedience to it. In harmonious concurrence, the will was naturally instructed to obey God. There was at that time no discordance or possibility of disruption among the faculties so long as the initial state of righteousness was preserved.[25]

A highly significant sense exists, therefore, in which it can be said that at the fall man lost his free will. His intellectual faculty was henceforth blinded by the god of this world (2 Cor. 4:4; 1 Cor 2:14) and his emotional faculty was enslaved by the devil to the extent that he was

---

22. See Murray, "Progressive Sanctification" in *Collected Writings*, vol. 2, 294–304.
23. See Vickers, *The Immediacy of God*, chaps. 3–5.
24. Westminster Shorter Catechism, Question 13, italics added.
25. See the discussion in Cunningham, on "The Doctrine of the Will," in *Historical Theology*, vol. 1, 568–639.

now a God-hater (Rom 1:30). Because with the mind man could no longer *know* God and the good that God required, and because with the heart now turned from God and enslaved to sin he could not *love* the good, the mind and the heart could no longer instruct the will to *do* the good. That was the sorry state to which Adam and his posterity were reduced by his dereliction from what God's covenant had required of him. We have seen that as a result of the fall man is disabled from the initial functions and prerogatives with which he was created. But as to action in general, and apart from the precise question of the knowledge of God and actions in accordance with the mandates of the law of God, the question persists whether there exists any respect in which the will can be said to be free.

Our response must be that in all respects, and by the very nature of the constitution of the soul and human personhood, the will remains under the inevitable influence of the intellectual and emotional deliberations. When Jonathan Edwards said that the action of the will is "as the greatest apparent good is,"[26] he was laying down a principle which, of necessity, is universally explanatory of willing action. For example, a man may well have decided at one time or another that excessive consumption of alcohol is a thing which, on the basis of his own established moral principles, he will avoid. But if, on a certain occasion, he takes alcohol to an excess and thereby defies what he had previously laid down as a moral principle, it is not to be said that he is doing so against his will. Nor can it properly be said that his will is free, in an isolated and independent sense, to take the alcohol or not take it. The situation in strict reality is that he took the alcohol because, at the point of taking it, it was apparent to him that in the situation that then existed that action was seen as "his greatest apparent good." His reason and his emotional preferences at that time dictated that the preponderance of good rested in the action he then took. The action of taking the alcohol was not an independent act of the will. It was an act of the whole person.

What has just been said finds precise application in the ministry of the Spirit of God to and in the Christian life. While the will is free from outside compulsion, and while an individual cannot be forced to do something he does not will to do, nevertheless it is necessarily subject to the internal faculties of the soul in the manner we have seen, and, it can now be said, is subject to the mysterious supervision and direction of

---

26. Edwards, *Freedom of the Will*, 86.

the will of God. For in the will of God, and under the control of the sovereign ordering of God, all of the forces of history and the formation of character that bear on the formation and functioning of an individual's faculties transmit their effects, impulses, and determinations to the will and its actions.

But there is an aspect of freedom to which we hold in the Christian life. The members of the Galatian church to whom the apostle wrote were under pressure from certain teachers to come under the umbrella of a mistaken interpretation of the gospel. It was being said to them that they were quite correct in their claim that they must believe in Christ for salvation. That was quite true. But, the false teachers argued, it was not enough. It was said that those who committed themselves to Christ must also be circumcised. That is to say, they must become Jews, because entry to the Christian faith must be by way of Judaism.

What we see there is that a perversion of the gospel can present itself in two ways. In the first case, the error might be the elimination from the gospel message of what it should properly contain. That was essentially the error against which the Reformers of the sixteenth century had to take a forthright stand. The Roman church at that time, as continues to be the case at present, said that justification was by grace and faith in Christ. But they did not say, and on the basis of their semi-Pelagian construction of biblical doctrine they could not say, that justification was by faith in Christ *alone*. The deletion of the word *alone* made all the difference to what was said to be the gospel. It is true that the Roman Catholic understanding of the gospel was erroneous on other accounts also. While it agreed that salvation was by grace, it was wrongly claimed that it was by grace *infused* into the soul, not by the righteousness of Christ freely *imputed* to the believer. The Roman church had confused justification and sanctification.

The error in the statement of the gospel might, on the other hand, be the reverse of what has just been said. It might be a matter of adding to the gospel something that is not properly contained in it. We saw an instance of that when we observed that some theologians have argued that one is saved by "obedient faith," thereby inserting into the gospel statement the suggestion that one is justified, not by faith alone, but by faith plus the works of obedience.

Against the possibility that the Galatian church might be led astray by the false claims of the Judaisers, Paul said: "Stand fast therefore in the liberty wherewith Christ hath made us free, and be not entangled again with the yoke of bondage" (Gal 5:1). For there is a new liberty in the life that the believer now has in Christ. Paul's expressive language in referring to the false teaching as a "yoke of bondage" recalls the words of Christ himself. On a notable occasion he had declared to certain Jews who had protested belief in him that "If ye continue in my word, then are ye my disciples indeed; And ye shall know the truth, and the truth shall make you free" (John 8:31–32). But the Jews rebelled against the notion of the necessity of any new freedom. For as "Abraham's seed," they said, they "were never in bondage to any man" (John 8:33). The idea of bondage was an alien concept to them. But our Lord had spoken of their bondage to sin.

Paul had made the point in his letter to the Romans: "To whom ye yield yourselves servants [Greek: 'slaves'] to obey, his servants [slaves] ye are to whom ye obey; whether of sin, unto death, or of obedience unto righteousness. . . . ye were the servants of sin, but . . . Being then made free from sin, ye became the servants [Greek: 'ye were enslaved'] of righteousness" (Rom 6:16–18). Paul is saying there the same thing he said to the Galatians. There is a new liberty in Christ. But the issue is properly stated in a way that makes it clear that one is either enslaved to sin or enslaved to Christ. That is the paradox of Christian freedom. The Christian believer is now no longer in bondage to sin, because he is in bondage to Christ. What it amounts to is that now, in life in Christ Jesus, we are free to obey the law of God that otherwise condemns us. The Christian believer, in bondage to Christ by virtue of his new and indissoluble union with Christ, is now free to know God for who he is as revealed in Christ, free to serve him, and free to live in such a way as to be pleasing to him.

That new freedom has significance for what has been said of the individual believer's progress in sanctification. God works, and man works. In the matter of justification and reconciliation with God, the working of God in the individual's life did not amount to a synergism or in any sense a cooperative work. In that case there is not, and there could not be, any possibility of synergism, because at the time of the coming of the renewing grace of God the individual is "dead in trespasses and sins" (Eph 2:1). But in the present case of progress in sanctification, the Christian is called upon to play his part in obedience to the law of God and in the mortification of the principle of sin within him. The Christian person in the discharge of his ethical responsibilities that point to his sanctification is, as has now been said, decidedly under the supervision, direction, and support of the Holy Spirit.

Sanctification, then, is both the work of the individual and the work of the Spirit of God. In the ways we have seen, the Christian believer works because the Spirit of God works within him. Thus it is that "accepting, receiving, and resting upon Christ alone" results in the blessings of "justification, sanctification, and eternal life." And, in and with that, a new freedom in Christ Jesus exists.

5

The Refuge of the Cross

THE APOSTLE'S DECLARATION, "GOD forbid that I should glory, save in the cross of our Lord Jesus Christ" (Gal 6:14), was for him a complete reversal of all previous thought-constructs and life allegiances. His arrest on the road to Damascus evoked his response: "Who art thou, Lord?" (Acts 9:5). The meaning of the intervention of the "light from heaven" was not immediately clear. Nor was the identity of the speaker. Certainly, something that was blinding, not only in its effects on Paul's physical sight but on whatever interpretive categories he had been accustomed to conjure, had occurred. The apostle's "who art thou, Lord?" did not immediately invoke the name of the Lord God of heaven. His response indicates simply that he was conscious that he was addressed by a superhuman being. It might have been an angel. Paul did not know. It was therefore with a dramatic shock of self-realization that he heard the words, "I am Jesus whom thou persecutest." We do not, and we cannot, explore at length or speculate about the precise psychology of Paul's self-realization at that time. But there are some things of which we can be sure.

First, it is clear, as became apparent in the sequel, that on that occasion the Holy Spirit of God had arrested a man who, in spite of all his claims of self-knowledge and self-satisfaction, was being called to see himself as a sinner. Indeed, he was later to refer to himself as the chief of sinners (1 Tim 1:15). On the Damascus road that day we see the regenerating work of the Holy Spirit in the soul. We have said that the conveyance to a sinner of the grace of regeneration involves a sovereign, secret, and unsolicited work of the Spirit of God. If ever we needed a biblical confirmation, we have it in the record of the apostle's Damascus road arrest. What occurred that day was completely beyond the bounds of Paul's contemplation and quite outside the limits of what he had any reason to imagine was possible.

Second, the precise circumstances of the Holy Spirit's intervention in Paul's case do not establish a pattern for the Spirit's work in all people since. But we have in Paul's experience an indication of the Spirit's working that is his normal, necessary, and usual procedure. We do well to separate the precision and particularities of Paul's experience from the principles that are exemplified by the events he has recorded. We have in that record an illustration of what is involved in a soul's transition from wrath to grace, a translation from the kingdom of darkness to the kingdom of God's dear Son. In the first place, the arrest of the soul involves, as in Paul's case, a conviction of unworthiness and sin in the presence of God. That conviction carries with it the call to recognize that the explanation of our condition necessarily begins with the awareness that we stand before a holy God. The realization dawns on the soul that the root explanation of our condition is that hitherto we have lived our lives in such a way that we have been an offense to the holiness of God. That is always, and must necessarily be, the beginning of the process of conversion, to become aware of the shattering realization that as sinful people we have to do with a holy God.

If, then, as again in the case of Paul, the conviction of sin that presses on the soul is honestly entertained, it must lead to a totalitarian submission to Christ who has arrested us by his Spirit. Now that we know that we are in the presence of God who has called us, now that we hear, with a newness that before was foreign to us, that Christ himself calls us with his "come unto me" (Matt 11:28), we see also that he is demanding of us a totalitarian commitment and allegiance. For the realization matures that it is only in union with him that true life consists. And then it becomes clear to us, as with Paul, that God responds to our acknowledgment and confession and tells us what we must do. As to one of old whom the Spirit of God unexpectedly brought to the same realization, the instruction and call is: "Believe on the Lord Jesus Christ, and thou shalt be saved" (Acts 16:31). Moreover, the call of Christ impresses its verity on the soul when he says: "and I will give you rest" (Matt 11:28).

The Spirit of God works in ways of his sovereign choosing in the lives and consciousness of those to whom the gospel is announced. In many instances, the Spirit's convicting work may continue to very great and even extreme lengths, and yet not be consummated in conveying to the sinner the grace of regeneration. A biblical instance of precisely that is contained in the sixth chapter of the letter to the Hebrews. Certain people there were to a degree "once enlightened . . . tasted of the heavenly gift . . . partakers of the Holy Ghost . . . tasted the good word of God, and the powers of the world to come" (Heb 6:4–5). Yet they remained unregenerate, they were still in their sins, and as the writer to the Hebrews states: "It is impossible . . . if they shall fall away, to renew them again unto repentance; seeing they crucify to themselves the Son of God afresh, and put him to an open shame" (Heb 6:4, 6). What is being said is that if certain false professors, whom God in his sovereign, covenantal purpose has not brought to true faith in Christ, should recant their profession, it is not possible to renew them even to the false profession they had previously made.[1]

Why, when the call of Christ is announced in the gospel, does not the response that Paul made rise in every person's heart? Paul's status of soul as he set out on his journey to Damascus provides us with aspects of the answer and explanation. But let us see the question in its most general terms. The first thing to be said, of course, consistent with all we have discussed in earlier contexts, is illustrated starkly by the words of our Lord himself. Again, the heart of what has been eternally purposed in the Covenant of Grace comes into perspective. "At the time Jesus answered and said, I thank thee, O Father, Lord of heaven and earth, because thou hast hid these things from the wise and prudent, and hast revealed them unto babes" (Matt 11:25). It is not necessary to recall at this point all that has been said regarding the terms and objectives of the Covenant of Grace. Suffice it to say that we have already seen that those who do not come to Christ do not because they will not. Those will come, we have seen, to whom the Spirit of God gives the grace of regeneration that carries with it the gifts of repentance and faith that Christ purchased for his people.

What is it, then, about the human condition apart from that renewing grace of God that prevents the natural man from turning to Christ? First, to respond most generally, the reason is that all men by nature have shared in Adam's assertion of autonomy from God. That was the essence of Adam's fall. Although he knew that he had come from the hands of

---

1. Some commentators understand the Hebrews text differently. Sproul, for example, based on an apparent misunderstanding of the "repentance" referred to in the text, concludes that "the author is describing regenerate Christians." *Grace Unknown*, 214.

God, though he knew that he was under covenantal obligations to God, his false assertion of autonomy meant that he would not live out his life in accordance with the criteria of belief and behavior that God had revealed to him. His false and damning assertion of autonomy came to expressions on the levels of being, knowledge, and behavior. Metaphysically, or, that is, as to his being, he would deny his Creator's explanation and revelation. Epistemologically, or as to the criteria of truth and validity in knowledge, he would henceforth find those criteria from within himself and his own imaginations or in the cultural milieu in which he lived. On the level of ethics, or moral behavior, he would again turn aside from the rules of rightness that God had given him. Our first parent, against his better self-awareness and pristine God-consciousness, effectively denied his creaturehood and its implications and mandates on all the three levels, of being, belief, and behavior. That, precisely, is the bequest that has descended to all of his natural posterity.

The second reason for refusing to come to Christ is a natural result of the assertion of autonomy. It is the pride of life that accompanies the claim that one is, in the ways we have observed, sufficient unto himself. The pride of life comes to expression in many different ways. The apostle John spoke of it in the broadest of terms. "Love not the world, neither the things that are in the world. If any man love the world, the love of the Father is not in him" (1 John 2:15). Our Lord has said the same thing: "Lay not up for yourselves treasures upon earth . . . For where your treasure is, there will your heart be also" (Matt 6:19, 21). The pride of life that cuts men off from Christ is, in other words, a worldly mindedness. In an age that has become materialistic in the extreme, men have made gods of things. The love of men has turned in upon themselves and away from God, and it follows that they have made gods for themselves in their own image. The gods they have made vary with the individual. They may be material—houses, lands, possessions; they may be cultural—associations, families, social alignments; they may be personal—careers, ambitions, and any number of expressions of self-centeredness. In short, having turned from God, men have become a law unto themselves. The apostle Paul spoke eloquently to the facts in the first chapter of his letter to the Romans (Rom 1:18–32).

Thirdly, the general obstacle of the pride of life comes to particular expression in what was no doubt the case with Paul (Saul) before his arrest on the road to Damascus. That is the pride of intellect. That follows in yet a different way from the natural man's assertion of autonomy. It is the pride of saying that the human intellect is capable of understanding all things on the basis of unaided human reason. In our first chapter we took brief account of the elevation of the supposed competence of human reason in what Descartes had advanced at the beginning of modern philosophy and which came to culmination in the so-called Enlightenment of the eighteenth century. It was at the end of that century that Immanuel Kant appeared and rewrote philosophic epistemology (the theory of knowledge) in a way that has had rippling influences ever since. It has not left the theology of the church untouched.

Paul, educated at the feet of Gamaliel, was beyond doubt of the aristocracy of intellect, learned in the laws of the Pharisees and in the philosophies of the times, as evidenced by his address at the Areopagus recorded in the seventeenth chapter of the book of Acts. But he learned to say that "what things were gain to me, those I counted loss for Christ. Yea doubtless, and I count all things but loss for the excellency of the knowledge of Christ Jesus my Lord; for whom I . . . count them but dung, that I may win Christ" (Phil 3:7-8). Paul learned to say: "Beware lest any man spoil you [lead you astray and make you captive] through philosophy and vain deceit, after the tradition of men, after the rudiments of the world, and not after Christ" (Col 2:8). If any man had been able to be justly proud of intellect it was the apostle Paul. But for him that counted as nothing, in the light of what was to be gained in obedience to Christ.

The next reason why men do not naturally come to Christ rests in many instances on a different level. That has to do with the fact that as a result of Adam's fall and the bequest we have seen it projected to all men since, the faculties of the soul have been disordered and depraved. In Adam's initial state of holiness and righteousness the mind, the intellectual faculty, was the prince of the faculties of the soul. Adam naturally knew God, he naturally loved and sought after God, and he naturally obeyed the law of God with a ready determination to be pleasing to God. But now, as we have explained more fully already, the hegemony of the mind has been usurped by the emotions and the passions of the affective faculty. Man has turned from a natural love of God to make himself a God-hater. He has turned inward upon himself and now that there is no law of God before his eyes he is a god unto himself. He cannot turn to Christ in response to the call of the gospel apart from the revivifying initiative of the Holy Spirit in his soul, because every aspect of his life, desires, and imaginations is pointed to his own indulgence and away from God.

The assumption of autonomy, the pride of life, the pride of intellect, and his natural self-absorption keep the natural man from Christ. But we should note further Paul's statement that he *gloried* in the cross of Christ. It is to be observed that for the natural man, the things we have so far noted not only keep him from Christ, but he actually *glories* in them. That is what is involved in his having made a god of them. We have observed in earlier contexts that by reason of man's creation as the image of God there naturally resides in the human soul a *sensus deitatis*, a sense of God by which all men know that God is. But we say also that embedded within the soul is a *semen religionis*, a seed of religion. Man, by nature, must worship. He is, essentially and by creation, a religious being. He will live by either a godly religion or an ungodly religion. He will worship the true God or he will worship gods of his own making. In the progress of thought it has been said, with some condescension perhaps, that religion is legitimately a part of culture. But, we say, the contrary is true. Culture is part of religion. By that we mean that man is naturally a religious being in the sense we have seen, he must naturally worship some one or other god, and the culture he develops will naturally and inevitably be a religious culture. The reality is that it will either be a godly culture whose determining structures are grounded in godly assumptions and presuppositions, or it will be a godless culture. That the latter has developed in the extreme in these current times is beyond argument to the reflective Christian mind.

The next reason why the natural man does not come to Christ, then, is that by nature he is an idolater. That was a part of God's principal complaint against his people in the Old Testament administration of the Covenant of Grace. The repeated complaints of the prophets were pointed to the twofold sins of spiritual adultery and idolatry. Indeed, the prophet Jeremiah joins those two sins together in a most interesting way. "I saw," God says, "when for all the causes whereby backsliding Israel committed adultery I had put her away, and given her a bill of divorce; yet her treacherous sister Judah feared not, but went and played the harlot also. And it came to pass through the lightness of her whoredom, that she defiled the land, and *committed adultery with stones and with sticks*" (Jer 3:8–10, italics added). God had chosen Israel as the nation from which the promised Messiah would come, they belonged to him, he had established his true church among them, but in their spiritual adultery they turned away from him and served other gods. The true measure of their idolatry was that in it they were worshiping false gods.

So it has been ever since. The natural man, who remains, notwithstanding Adam's fall, the image of God and continues to sustain covenantal obligations to God, has left himself without the knowledge of the true God and has joined himself to idols. His idols are born of his own self-directed and false conceptions and imaginations and lusts. It is apposite that at the end of his first epistle, the apostle John entreated his readers: "Little children, keep yourselves from idols" (1 John 5:21). What it comes to is that man does not naturally seek God; he will not naturally respond to the call to come to Christ because he is, as he imagines, comfortable in himself.

THE REFUGE OF THE CROSS

But there is an ache at the heart of modern man. The fashion of the times is to say that we live in a postmodern age. But however the contemporary culture is construed, there is an emptiness, a void, a gnawing of conscience which, when a reflective moment intervenes in the rush of life, leaves the individual person with an awareness that he has not discovered true satisfaction. He finally does not have any conviction that in his numbed conformity with the mores, tastes, and habits of the world he has discovered any true meaning for his life. The sense of eternity disturbs him. He numbs it rather than face it. In the words of the apostle, he suppresses every wakening awareness of the being and the claims of God (Rom 1:18). The natural man is at sea, in an ocean he cannot define and whose limits are beyond his comprehension, wrestling in his leaky craft with the crush of waves that crash with deceptive force upon him. They portend an untimely end. Eternity beckons him, but the haven to which he moves, dark for him in its indistinctness, generates only a foreboding.

The age, it is said, is postmodern. It is beyond our purposes to examine the meaning of all of the new vocabulary and its applications. At a minimum, and for its relevance to our diagnosis of the human condition apart from the grace of God, the following can be said. The so-called age of modernism spanned from the middle of the seventeenth century to roughly the middle of the twentieth century or slightly beyond, though there were crumblings toward the latter end of that period, in the fashion of existentialism, for example, in the earlier twentieth century. While there are obviously grave dangers of misrepresentation and misunderstanding of detail in painting with such a broad brush in the history of thought, it can be said that the main characteristic of modernism was its assumption of the competence of human reason. We took note of that earlier in our reference to the beginnings of modern philosophy and its expansion through the Enlightenment of the eighteenth century. Modernism assumed, in short, that it was within the competence of unaided reason to achieve an understanding of all things and to establish criteria of truth on all levels of explanation. That changed dramatically with the coming of postmodernism.

Modernism as an identifiable movement in the history of thought had imagined that it was within the scope of human reason to establish absolute criteria of meaning and truth even if, as has been said, those absolutes were grounded in nothing outside of the reaches of human reason, and even if they were to be approached with gradualness and, to take a phrase from D. A. Carson, asymptotically.[2] It was assumed that if only it were given time and effort, human reason could know and understand everything. That is an aspect of the claim that the only difference between the knowledge that God possesses and man's knowledge is quantitative. What we have seen as the qualitative difference is ignored or denied. But now in postmodernism, there are no absolutes. Now there is no longer any definitive and absolute truth that is attainable at the end of the search for meaning or that influences that search itself. There are now only truths. Any individual's truth is as good as any other individual's truth. The only permissible absolute is the statement that there are no absolutes. Indeed, some of the expressions of postmodernism have gone so far as to argue that it cannot now be said that there exists any continuity of human personhood and character. The individual is what his history of exposure to the random forces of change and circumstance make him to be. The elimination of continuity of personhood, it should be clear, leads to the destruction of ethics, because it points away from the ultimate moral responsibility of the individual. What has been achieved by that trajectory can be set beside an earlier development that

---

2. Carson, *Gagging of God*, 544. The literature on postmodernism, as it has come to expression in many of the learned disciplines, is too extensive to warrant any attempt at summary at this point. For an excellent insightful treatment see Carson, op. cit. See also Trueman, *Minority Report*, for insightful comments on the relation between contemporary evangelicalism and its "mere Christianity" and postmodernism.

had led to claims of the death of God. That, now, has been followed, in effect, by the death of man.

The defect of postmodernist thought is that there does not exist in relation to it any basic, determinative "metanarrative." By metanarrative we mean a fundamental and overarching statement of truth that gives form and meaning to what is said from that point on. We have seen that in consistently held biblical theology, a metanarrative exists in the form of the presupposition that God is, based on the revelation that God has given, and that at the root of meaning on all levels of human comprehension is the divine declaration of God's covenantal purpose.

Postmodernism has bred a new human arrogance. We hear in it the echo of what characterized the times at the end of the period of the Old Testament judges. "In those days . . . every man did that which was right in his own eyes" (Judg 21:25). Carson has reflected astutely on the developments: "Postmodernism gently applied rightly questions the arrogance of modernism; postmodernism ruthlessly applied nurtures a new hubris and deifies agnosticism."[3] In the postmodern age, man is lonely now. Not only is he without God, for God is dead, but he can no longer be sure of any ultimate or confidently assumed meaning of himself. That is the ironic result of his imagination that he was finally able to be all things to himself in his own sovereign way. The end result is the assumption of human autonomy gone wild and become mad.

Yet man cannot escape from God who is man's environment, "in whom we live, and move, and have our being" (Acts 17:28), and God confronts him at the times and in the ways God sovereignly chooses. At the same time, while every man remains accountable to God, he does, in spite of himself, do things that accord with the law of God. He does that, not from any motivation to acknowledge and please God, but because there remains within him the shadow of the "old man," the old prelapsarian Adamic man. As the apostle explained in his letter to the Romans, the works of the law of God are written in his heart. Observe the apostle's argument: "When the Gentiles, which have not the law, do by nature the things contained in the law, these, having not the law, are a law unto themselves: which show *the work of the law written in their hearts*" (Rom 2:14–15, italics added). The unregenerate person does not have the law of God written in his heart. That was surrendered when Adam fell. They, Paul says, "having not the law, are a law unto them-

---

3. Carson, *Gagging of God*, 544.

selves." The text says that it is not the *law* that is written in the heart, but the *works of the law*. The difference is significant. It raises the question of why, in spite of themselves and in spite of their unregenerate character, individuals do things that are socially good and, on the surface of things, consistent with the second table of the law. Not all men murder. Not all steal. Many are honest in word and in relations with other people. Many exhibit a love for fellow creatures. How should that be so? The answer is not that the law of God is written in their heart as an infallible motivation to behavior. The facts are different. Notwithstanding Adam's fall and the inheritance of sinful nature that descended on all men as a result, the sense of God remains within them, and though, as the text says, they have constructed their own law, the memory of paradise remains; and by the development of God's common grace, a moral sensitivity to right and wrong that is inherent in the soul is developed to greater or lesser degrees. There is in every person a residual memory of the law of righteousness as it was given to Adam in the first place, shadowy and indistinct though that residue may be.

But for the torn and tortured reality of the human condition, it is the glory of the gospel of the grace of God to announce that there is refuge in the cross of Christ. It is against the lostness and the pain of self-realization of the human condition that Christ calls: "Come unto me . . . and I will give you rest" (Matt 11:28). There is a wideness of mercy in the cross of Christ. The prophet Isaiah had said: "Ho, every one that thirsteth, come ye to the waters" (Isa 55:1), foreseeing that when Christ, the Messiah, came he would give the water of life freely to those who believed on him. And in due time our Lord stated to a woman at the well in Samaria: "whosoever drinketh of the water that I shall give him shall never thirst; but the water that I shall give him shall be in him a well of water springing up into everlasting life" (John 4:14). The plea of Christ to sinners who are burdened and heavy laden by their sin and their search for true meaning continues to ring down through the ages. It is restated and confirmed in the very final paragraph of the final book of the Scriptures: "Let him that heareth say, Come. And let him that is athirst come. And whosoever will, let him take the water of life freely" (Rev 22:17).

The cross of Christ is the refuge from the penalty and the curse of sin because in the cross, the Scriptures announce, Christ is "made a curse for us" (Gal 3:13). The cross of Christ declares the wideness of

God's mercy, and it opens wide the doors of the kingdom of God to all who will believe in him. The apostle's text at Galatians 3:13-14 speaks eloquently to the objectives of the Covenant of Grace. The argument of the context warrants close inspection.

The first question to be asked is: Who is it the apostle has in mind in his statement that "Christ hath redeemed *us* from the curse of the law" (Gal 3:13)? Or again, what is the "law" from which they have been redeemed? And if the "us" forms in the mind of the apostle a restricted class of people, as will be seen to be the case, what is said in the context of benefits to men in general by virtue of the redemptive work of Christ? It is clear from a close inspection of the context that the apostle is drawing a distinction between the status of the Jews to whom the Mosaic law had been given and the status and potential salvation of the rest of mankind. In the tenth verse of the chapter Paul had spoken of the curse accruing to those who are "of the works of the law," for "cursed is every one that continueth not in all things *which are written in the book of the law* to do them" (italics added). The "book of the law" that Paul refers to there is clearly the law of Moses. That law had been given to Israel but it had not been given to the Gentiles, and the apostle is accordingly distinguishing between those of the Jews who are "redeemed from the curse of the law" as it had been given, on the one hand, and, on the other, the Gentiles to whom he will go on to refer. The Gentiles, not having been given the law, "could not be considered to be exposed to *its* curse, and, of course, they could not be represented as redeemed from a curse to which they were never subject."[4]

On those grounds, John Brown, writing in the early nineteenth century, has concluded convincingly that the "us," therefore refers to "those Jews who had become Christians."[5] It would therefore not be appropriate, as has frequently been done in the history of commentary, to assume that when it is said that Christ hath redeemed us from the curse of the law the "us" has reference, *in the context now in view*, to all of God's elect people. We have seen the "us" to refer to a class of people, namely believing Jews. There is no doubt, of course, that in the present context the expiatory, penal, and propitiatory efficacy of the substitutionary sacrifice of Christ is fully in view. But what, we may then ask, is to be understood of the redemption by the death of Christ of those

---

4. Brown, *Galatians*, 129-30.
5. Ibid., 130.

outside of the Jews? Does the Scripture *in this context* contemplate any benefit for sinners outside of Jewry? The answer is most decidedly "Yes." And the continuation of Paul's argument is pointed to that effect in such a way that it exhibits in remarkably economical terms the saving intention of the Covenant of Grace.

In the death of Christ, it is being said, the curse of the old Mosaic law was paid for and satisfied. All of the types and anticipations of the redeemer that were integral to the earlier administration had been fulfilled in Christ. The meaning of that, in turn, was that as all of the promises to the Jews of the coming of the Messiah-Redeemer had been fulfilled, the doors of the kingdom could now be thrown wide open to the Gentiles. That is precisely what the apostle envisages. He goes on to say that the design or consequence of Christ's redeeming Jewish believers from the curse of the law was that "the blessing of Abraham might come on the Gentiles" (Gal 3:14). That blessing for Gentile believers would be the same as accrued to the Jewish believers, namely justification from the guilt of sin and adoption into the family of God by reason of their union with Christ.

We have adduced the foregoing exegesis of the Galatian text in order to impress on ourselves again the full significance of the saving work of Christ in his sacrificial death on the cross. John Brown sums up the significance of what is in view in the apostle's argument by observing: "Christ's endurance of the curse of the Mosaic law in the room of such of his people as were subject to it, was the honourable and appropriate termination of that economy which, while it continued, presented insurmountable obstacles to 'the blessing of Abraham,' or justification by believing, being generally extended to the Gentiles."[6] Brown continues: "The peculiar relation in which God stood to one nation as his own people must be dissolved in order to the formation of a covenant relation with a peculiar people, which was to consist of persons of all nations."[7] The letter to the Hebrews establishes the point by stating that "he taketh away the first [the Mosaic covenant] that he may establish the second" (Heb 10:9). Because of that development of God's covenant it could be said, as did the apostle John, that "he [Christ] is the propitiation for our sins: and not for ours only, but also for the sins of the whole world" (1 John 2:2). John is not saying there that the benefits of the death of Christ

6. Ibid., 134–35.
7. Ibid., 135.

extend to all men in the sense that his atonement was a universal or indiscriminate atonement. We have already seen that the Covenant of Grace contemplates a particular, not a universal, atonement, and that its benefits extend to God's elect. John's statement is not addressed to the extent of the atonement. It is addressed to the excellence and the infinite worth of the one who was the propitiation for sin. Wherever, that is, from among the Jews and the Gentiles, any person's sins are propitiated, it is the one propitiator, Jesus Christ, who by his death on the cross is the Savior from sin.

We have said that the promises of the Mosaic economy and covenant were fulfilled in the death of Christ. The curse of the Mosaic law had been satisfied. But that in no sense is to be taken as saying that the law of God has no longer any relevance to the life of Christian believers. The law of God as given through Moses is to be understood in its threefold aspects of the ceremonial, the civil or judicial, and the moral law. The law in its ceremonial aspect was fulfilled in Christ because he was, as has been said, the antitype of the types that pointed to him and anticipated him in the Old Testament administration. In particular, Christ, as the great high priest who was to come, was the antitype of which the Levitical priesthood was typical. That fact is displayed copiously in the letter to the Hebrews and is, in fact, a principal motif of that letter. The law in its civil and institutional aspect was similarly terminated in the coming of Christ, except, as the Westminster Confession states it, for "the general equity thereof."[8] But the law in its moral aspect, as it has been encapsulated in the Ten Commandments, remains the rule of life for God's people. In that aspect, the law is to be seen as a republication and rearticulation of the law of righteousness that God gave to Adam at the beginning. Because the law in that aspect is a restatement of creation ordinances, it is binding on all men generally, everywhere, and at all times.

It can properly be said, without any contradiction of what we have inspected as the argument of the apostle in the letter to the Galatians, that Christ on the cross was made a curse for all of God's chosen people. All of his people were redeemed by the cross of Christ from the curse that devolved on them by reason that they had repudiated the demands of God's holy law. But what, we ask, was the law that was involved? For the Jews that law was the Mosaic law in its unique and particular expressions, ceremonial, civil, and moral. For the Gentiles it was the law

---

8. Westminster Confession of Faith, XIX:4.

of God's righteousness as initially promulgated when God had created Adam and conveyed to him the terms of his covenant and probation. It could therefore be properly said that "all have sinned, and come short of the glory of God" (Rom 3:23). There is none righteous. Not one.

God's covenantal design was such that he gave his law to his people of old in order that it might be a "schoolmaster to bring [them] unto Christ" (Gal 3:24). The import of the text is not primarily to the effect, as it has frequently been interpreted, that the law was given as a means of convicting us of sin in order that, as a result, we might be brought to Christ. That that effect of the law is operative is, of course, true, as is elsewhere stated: "by the law is the knowledge of sin" (Rom 3:20). But in the Galatian context, the law was a schoolmaster to God's people, the nation-church of Israel, in that it was given to them to hedge them in from all the nations of the world, and to preserve them in the darkness of sin and estrangement from God that otherwise existed, in order that Christ should come from them. When Christ had come, Paul then says to the Galatians, "we are no longer under a schoolmaster" (Gal 3:25). The schoolmaster office and function of the law had been fulfilled.

But the objectives of the Covenant of Grace had, in it all, been fulfilled in Christ's going to the cross. For then, as not only the Jews but also the Gentiles had become the beneficiaries of "the blessing of Abraham" (Gal 3:14), all of the redeemed, Jews and Gentiles, were together "Abraham's seed, and heirs according to the promise" of the Covenant of Grace (Gal 3:29).

THE REFUGE OF THE CROSS IN THE CHRISTIAN LIFE

The cross holds out to all mankind a broad and efficient refuge. It is a refuge to the sinner who, awakened by the Spirit of God to a sense of his sin, knows that he stands in need of a refuge which, the gospel declares, is provided only in the abounding merit of the cross of Christ. The cross is a refuge to the saint who has sinned, the child of God who is again burdened by the realization of his failure and his fall, of having dishonored his Lord and Savior and having, by his actions or imaginations, grieved the Holy Spirit of God. The cross is a refuge to the child of God who is burdened by temptation to sin.

We took note in an earlier chapter of the fact that in the grace of regeneration that brings the sinner to Christ the process of sanctification has begun. Now, as we reflect further on the refuge of the cross, the meaning and message of the cross speak loudly to the Christian life. The apostle John has struck to the heart of the matter in the first paragraph of his first epistle. He writes, he says, "that ye also may have fellowship with us: and truly *our fellowship is with the Father*, and with his Son Jesus Christ" (1 John 1:3, italics added). The astounding reality of the benefits conferred on those whom Christ redeemed by his cross is that union with him carries with it union with the blessed three Persons of the Godhead. But the fellowship with the Father that is here announced as the believer's privilege is to be jealously guarded. For consider what it is that falls incumbently upon him. "If we say that we have fellowship with him [God the Father], and walk in darkness, we lie, and do not the truth" (1 John 1:6). Sin, it is regrettably necessary to say, continues in the life of the believer. We have looked at its reason and origin and at what John Owen referred to as the "contrary habitual principle," or what Dabney called the *habitus* or disposition to sin that remains in the regenerate person. Without rehearsing what has already been said to that effect, the apostle now turns our thought and conscience to the cross of Christ.

"If we walk in the light, as he is in the light," John says, "we have fellowship one with another, and the blood of Jesus Christ his Son cleanseth us from all sin" (1 John 1:7). Two things are at issue. First, John has carefully constructed the context within which he is writing. He has said that "God is light," thereby stating at the foundation of his argument that God is a holy God. Going on to explain the necessity that God's people should live in holiness and righteousness before him, he is saying that the sin into which the believer can fall breaks the blessedness of the realization of that fellowship. Second, when he states that "we have fellowship one with another," the fellowship he is speaking about is again the fellowship between God and the believer. Robert Candlish, one of the leaders of the famous disruption of the Scottish Presbyterian church in 1843 that led to the formation of the Free Church of Scotland, has judiciously observed: "'We have fellowship one with another;' God with us and we with God. For it is not our mutual fellowship as believers amongst ourselves that is meant; the introduction of that idea is irrelevant, and breaks the sense. It is our joint-fellowship with God, and his with us, that alone is to the purpose here."[9]

The Christian sins. That has been well established. But what, then, is in view in the apostle's argument as the necessary preservative of the

---

9. Candlish, *1 John*, 47–48.

fellowship with God of which he has spoken? He well says that "if we confess our sins, he [God] is faithful and just to forgive us our sins, and to cleanse us from all unrighteousness" (1 John 1:9). But what, again, is the only efficient ground on which that forgiveness can be forthcoming? Here the cross of Christ towers above all the sins and disabilities and failures of those who were redeemed by the divine transaction that the cross effected. It is, John says, "the blood of Jesus Christ his Son [that] cleanseth us from all sin" (1 John 1:7). William Cowper's well-known hymn is to the point: "There is a fountain filled with blood, drawn from Immanuel's veins; / and sinners, plunged beneath that flood, lose all their guilty stains."[10] In his substitutionary death on the cross, Christ dealt definitively with the sin of those for whom he died. In the imputation to the repentant sinner of the righteousness of Christ the sins of his people were dealt with, their sins both in times that are past and in the days yet to come.

The apostle having made that clear to the Romans, what might be thought to be a logical deduction from it came immediately to the surface of his thought. If that is so, if the blood of Christ has dealt with sins that are past and is an atonement for sins that will follow in the future, what reason exists to avoid future sins? The horror of such a conclusion as is implied in the question came rapidly. "Shall we continue in sin, that grace may abound?" The only answer is: "God forbid. How shall we, that are dead to sin, live any longer therein?" (Rom 6:2). When it was said that Christ demands a totalitarian allegiance, the true believer's response is that by his grace and by the ministry to him of the Spirit of God he will strain every nerve to live honestly and righteously before God. In his new-found state of acceptance with God, the "love of Christ constrains him" (See 2 Cor 5:14).

The cross of Christ is a refuge not only for Christian believers who are conscious of the burden of sin, who are aware of their entrapment in occasions of sin. It is the refuge also for the child of God who is suffering from the pressure of temptation to sin. Paul had occasion to write on the matter to the Corinthian church, a church that was troubled with division and problems of immorality and pressures to conform to the life-patterns of the pagan world around it. In his "godly jealousy" for the Christians there he was, he said, fearful "lest by any means, as the serpent beguiled Eve through his subtlety, so your minds should be cor-

---

10. Cowper, *There Is a Fountain Filled with Blood*, 253.

rupted from the simplicity that is in Christ" (2 Cor 11:3). The Christian is to be alertly aware of the subtlety of the tempter. Paul observed in the same context that "Satan himself transforms himself into an angel of light" (2 Cor 11:14, NKJV). Temptation to sin does not always present itself or advertise itself as temptation. It is the subtlety of the whole matter that so frequently leads to difficulties in the Christian life. Sin does not always and clearly advertise itself to the Christian mind as sin. Though the thing in itself may be transparently repulsive to the alert and sensitive Christian, the subtlety of the forms in which sin, the opportunities for the occasions of sin, and the temptation to sin present themselves can all too easily take the Christian unawares.

Paul had said to the Corinthians that he feared their "minds should be corrupted." That, it should be clear, often takes us to the root of the problem of sin and temptation in the Christian life. In the presence of temptation to sin and the allurements of sin, something happens all too frequently to the Christian mind. It is the confusion and the disturbance of the mind, and of the clear sightedness with which it should persevere in guiding the Christian life, that raises the problem. We have characterized the state of the natural man in sin by saying that for him, the emotions and the passions of the affective faculty have usurped the hegemony of the mind as the prince of the faculties of the soul. But in the regenerate person the previously shattered state of the faculties has been remedied, a harmony is reestablished between the faculties, and the mind of the Christian is again set to guide his life and behavior. But in the case of the Christian's sin, the reality is that for that occasion and in so far as sin is entertained, the Christian has ceased to think christianly.

The apostle had addressed the matter from another point of view in his first letter to the Corinthians. He was forced to say to them that he could not write to them "as unto spiritual, but as unto carnal" people (1 Cor 3:1). He said that "ye are yet carnal" (1 Cor 3:3). Paul was not there telling the people that he regarded them as having fallen away irreparably from the standing and position they had attained by virtue of their Christian faith and their union with Christ. That was not at issue at all. The fact was that they were behaving *as though they were still carnal*. The problem was not that they had ceased to be Christians. The problem was that they had fallen into the entrapment of Satan and were as a result living far below the real and true position that they had occupied in Christ.

For all of the reasons we have seen, the first thing the Christian believer is to do is to understand the temptation to sin and the terrible subtlety of it, the ease with which the mind can be beguiled by it, and the danger that awaits the Christian soul as a result. It follows that an understanding of temptation depends on an understanding of sin. The Christian is rendered the more secure against the temptation to sin as he understands more acutely the meaning of sin itself. That, in turn, makes it clear that the cross of Christ provides the refuge in times of temptation, because the cross speaks to us of the unspeakable horror of sin. It was our sin that nailed our Lord to the cross. If, then, we grasp the enormity of what was involved in the divine exchange that occurred when Christ died for our sin, how can we be careless about the entertainment of sin? In an important sense the non-Christian, the unregenerate man, is not disturbed by temptation. He lives contentedly in his corruption in sin, because he has not yet a true understanding of the meaning of sin. He may suffer, to greater or lesser degrees, pangs of remorse because he has failed to live up to certain standards of morality that he has erected for himself. He sleeps his senseless sleep of pseudo-peace in the hands of the evil one of whom he is by nature the servant and slave.

There is undoubtedly a sincerity of regret that the noble sinner feels when he has failed to honor what moral code he has set for himself. But when we speak of the Christian's temptation to sin we are speaking of something much more profound and meaningful than mere regret at offending a code of conduct. But there is a further difficulty in the Christian's life as it affects and is affected by this important problem. That is that at stages of spiritual growth, most notably at earlier stages of the Christian life, certain life constructs, behavior patterns, and perhaps habitual indulgences may not appear as sin. Because, in such instances, sin is not seen for what it is, the concept of temptation to sin has not any operative meaning. It is again in such a condition that the cross of Christ is a refuge to which the Christian should be ever ready to repair. For it is as we survey the cross that the meaning of sin becomes clearer, and the significance and the shapes and forms of temptation to sin become transparently recognizable.

But the most disturbing and saddest condition of all remains. It is the case of the Christian who knows that sin is sin, who knows that occasions of sin are occasions of sin, and yet who for the moment manages to convince himself that they are not sin, or that they can with adequate reason be accommodated. That may be done out of an imagined necessity to accommodate certain societal or cultural expectations. The situation may also arise when the soul is in somewhat of a state of exhaustion following a period of particular blessedness or service in the cause of Christ. But there are times when the clearest understanding may be temporarily dulled, or when the judgment of the enlightened Christian conscience may be set aside, and the desires of the old man reassert themselves. That may occur even in the case of a Christian who, in the normal course of life, has enjoyed the purest and sincerest experience of a close walk with Christ and communion with him.

In all of the instances we have contemplated, the cross of Christ is the sure and safe refuge for sin and the temptation to sin. We can sum up what is involved by saying that the cross is the refuge for sinners who receive and believe for the first time the good news of the gospel; it is the refuge for Christians who experience the agony and anguish of soul in the knowledge that they have sinned; and it is the refuge for the Christian believer who, for any of a number of reasons, finds himself caught in the web of temptation. The Christian can come again and again, he must necessarily come again and again, to the cross of Christ where the Substitute for sinners paid to the full the price of sin.

6

The Sufficiency of the Cross

Two principal issues have motivated our discussions to this point. First, God, by reason of his omnipresence, is our environment, and in him we live and move and have our being. He has condescended to make a revelation of his being, will, and purpose in terms that are understandable to us in our finitude and sin and he has revealed himself as a covenant-making and covenant-keeping God. In the Scriptures he has said his last word to us and he has nothing to say to man that he has not already said. Second, the objectives of the divine Covenant of Redemption have been brought to effect in the cross of Christ. It was necessary that the eternal Son of God should come into this world and die for sinners, as the only means of redeeming and reconciling to himself those from out of the race of Adam and his posterity whom he has chosen to share his eternal kingdom of glory.

The details of the scriptural arguments that bear on those issues have been explored in summary, but not in completely expansive, terms. It is not necessary to recall them at length. But briefer references to two matters will draw together the principal threads of our discussions and will project the implications for the Christian life. We refer first, to the sufficiency of the cross and to the intercessory office of Christ that follows the cross; and second, to the imperatives for the Christian life that the cross projects.[1]

The conclusion the Scriptures announce is that the cross, with the divine transaction between the Father and the Son that occurred there, was sufficient to realize the ends that were designed in the Covenant of Redemption: the salvation of the people of God. By reason of the substitutionary sacrifice on the cross of the Messiah-Redeemer who, it had been promised throughout the ages, would come in the fullness of time,

---

1. Parts of this chapter are dependent on Vickers, *Bondage of Grace*.

the wrath of God against sin was appeased, divine justice was satisfied, and sinners were reconciled to God. The sufficiency of the cross to realize the ends in view is due to the excellence of the Person of Christ who went to the cross as our Redeemer. Only the sinless Prince of glory could carry the weight of the penalty of our sin. In the cross, the brightness and the brilliance of the love of God are set clearly against the blackness of sin that made the cross necessary. God loved his people from before the foundation of the world and sent his Son to be the propitiation for their sin (1 John 4:10). In the cross, the wisdom and mercy of God are displayed for angels and men to see. If we can measure the blackness of sin and the horror of the lostness and the "darkness for ever" (Jude 13) into which, apart from the grace of God, the first sin of Adam plunged us, then we can begin to measure the love of God in sending his Son to be our Redeemer. Or again, if we can measure the distance the eternal Son of God journeyed from the highest heaven to earth to deal with sin, then we can begin to measure both the love of God and the depth of sin that made the coming of our Redeemer necessary. God does not love us because Christ died for us. The reverse is true. Christ died for us because God loved us.

Let us put in a different way what has just been said. We observed in an earlier context that it has been properly remarked that the reference to the cross of Christ may be understood in a synecdochical sense. The reference to the cross, that is, may be taken to refer to Christ's redemptive work in its entirety, and thereby bring that entire work and its completion into view. That includes, as we are about to observe, our Lord's discharge of his heavenly high priestly office on our behalf. His high priestly office includes his intercession with the Father continuously for us. But, we ask, what does that intercession involve?

It is not that Christ prevails upon the Father to assume that we had never sinned. Nor is it that he prevails upon the Father to acknowledge that we have sinned but to overlook our sin and to take it as being true, therefore, that the punishment for sin can be deflected. Those possibilities cannot apply because it was precisely in order to bear the penalty for our sin that Christ came into the world. It is true that by reason that Christ bore the penalty of sin as our substitute and because the Father, in the sacrifice of his Son, has imputed the righteousness of Christ to us, he now looks on us *as though we had not sinned*. But when Christ brings us to the Father he knows that we have sinned, he acknowledges that we have sinned, and he freely agrees with the Father that we have sinned. But our High Priest in the heavens presents our case to the Father in the context of the divine recognition that because of the love for us that moved the Father to send his Son to redeem us, he is now presenting us to the Father as the ones for whose sin he has paid the perfect substitute penalty that the justice and the righteousness of God demanded.

Moreover, our great high priest and intercessor knows our need and our unnecessary anxiety, and he sympathizes with us in every condition. As he presents our case and our prayers to the Father, no good and necessary thing will the Father withhold from us who seek first his kingdom and his righteousness (Matt 6:33). He makes "all things work together for good to them that love God" (Rom 8:28). The Father set his love upon us and sent his Son into the world for our benefit (1 John 4:10). The only possible conclusion is not that in his intercession our Lord prevails upon the Father to love us because of what he has done for us, but that God has set forth Christ as our redeemer and intercessor precisely because he loved us. We may adduce again the words of the prophet Jeremiah that speak to the point: "I have loved thee with an everlasting love: therefore with lovingkindness have I drawn thee" (Jer 31:3). The fact of the love of God and the fact of the cross have come to confluence.

The sufficiency of the cross rests also in the definitiveness and the once-for-all sufficiency of the sacrifice that Christ made for sin. There is now no more offering for sin. The letter to the Hebrews concludes that Christ, "after he had offered one sacrifice for sins for ever, sat down on the right hand of God" (Heb 10:12). Paul stated to the Romans that Christ was "declared to be the Son of God *with power* . . . by the resurrection from the dead" (Rom 1:4, italics added). The "with power" alerts us to the fact that the status to which the Son of God was raised was in recognition of, and it was the reward for, the work of redemption that he had accomplished. In that, the Father denotes his satisfaction with the completed sacrificial work of Christ, and we have therein again the attestation of the sufficiency of the cross.

But the sufficiency of the cross is attested also, we have seen, by the declaration of the divine Son of God himself as to the definitiveness and sufficiency of his redemptive work. In his high priestly prayer to the Father on the night on which he was betrayed, and as he surveyed the cross that lay ahead, he stated: "I have finished the work which thou gavest me to do" (John 17:4). His claim that "I have finished the work," followed as it was by his "it is finished" (John 19:30) before he committed his (human) spirit to the Father on the cross, speaks to the sufficiency of the cross as accomplishing the ends designed in the eternal divine counsel. We recall the words of the prophet that had now been fulfilled: "He shall see of the travail of his soul, and shall be satisfied" (Isa 53:11). That assurance of sufficiency says to the sinning saint of God that it is in the cross that forgiveness, security, and comfort lie. We have seen that the cross is the refuge for sinners because by reason of it, as the hymn writer John Newton stated, the sinner can say: "I may my fierce accuser face, and tell him thou [Christ] hast died."[2]

It follows that the Spirit whom Christ has sent as his mediator to those whom he redeemed cannot leave them, joined as they now are to Christ. The Spirit knew from the beginning the turmoil and the traps, the temptations and the tests that the saints would face. He knew their fallings and their failings and their frequent faltering of faith. But though he knew that from the beginning, he nevertheless undertook the redemptive responsibility to conduct them to glory.

When we speak of the sufficiency of the cross to achieve the divine redemptive objectives, we should recognize that the infinite majesty and glory of the Person of the Redeemer imparts an infinite worth and value to the atonement he effected. By adducing the infinite value of the atonement we reject the notion that there existed a merely quantitative relation between, on the one hand, the penalty for sin that Christ bore and, on the other, the number of the elect for whom he died or the particular magnitude of their sins. Such a notion has appeared in the history of the church under the label of the commercial theory of the atonement. That theory suggests that if the number of the elect for whom Christ died had been different, or if the nature of their sin had been different, then the nature and the extent of the penalty that Christ bore would have been different. But adequate biblical data point in a vastly different direction. The death of Christ, it is clear, was a ransom for sin (Mark 10:45). Other so-called theories of the atonement have been advanced in the history of the church.[3] But the excellence of the Redeemer prevents any diminution of the value of the atonement below the infinite worth that it thereby possesses. The conclusion it is necessary to state is that

---

2. Newton, *Approach, My Soul, the Mercy Seat*, 507.

3. See Berkhof, *Systematic Theology*, 384–91.

the triune Godhead in its eternal council set forth a redemption that was brought to effect in the cross of Christ, infinitely sufficient for all that God intended in the Covenant of Redemption.

Moreover, any suggestion of proportionality between the extent of the penalty of the cross and the number of the redeemed or the nature of their sin fails to take adequate account of the meaning of sin. Sin, that is, in the affront it has given to the infinite holiness of God, attracts the infinite wrath of God and is in itself worthy of infinite damnation. Sinners are saved from infinite wrath by the infinite value of the atonement that was addressed to their condition by the infinite love of God. Of course, it might be asked why, if the cross of Christ is of infinite value, do not all people turn to the Christ of the cross for salvation. That any man is unsaved at last does not find its reason in a limitation of the power of the Christ of the cross to save. That any man is lost is not explained by any inadequacy in the value of the atonement for sin that was offered. We have seen in earlier contexts the explanation of what might be thought to be discrepancies in that respect. We have seen that the universal call of the gospel is rejected by many who do not come to Christ because they will not. They will not, unless the grace of God draws them (John 6:44).

We cannot diminish the import of the call of the gospel that "God so loved the world that he gave his only begotten Son, that whosoever believeth in him should not perish, but have everlasting life" (John 3:16). We are not being told, *in the context of that statement*, that God so loved the persons he had elected to make up his eternal kingdom. We are not being told that God so loved those he foreknew would come to Christ. We are being told that God so loved the world. He loved the world of men in general, and he gave his Son so that whosoever would come may come to him in repentance and faith in Christ. But as we have seen, the terrible inabilities and incapacities of sin are such that any man is saved, if he is saved, only by the grace and the effectual call of God. Our Lord's disciples on one occasion responded to his teaching about the difficulty of a man's detaching himself from his love of this world to come to Christ. In somewhat of perplexity they asked: "Who then can be saved?" The reply of our Lord is luminous in its import: "The things which are impossible with men," Christ responded, "are possible with God" (Luke 18:26–27).

We have said that the sufficiency of the cross, the efficiency of the cross to achieve the objectives that God intended, is correlated with the decrees of the divine counsel. A perfect consistency inheres in the relation between the redemptive design of the Godhead and the accomplishment of redemption by the cross of Christ. No atonement of greater value or worth could have been contemplated in the divine counsel. God went to the finally ununderstandable length, so far as our finite comprehension can conceive of it, that he "purchased the church with his own blood" (See Acts 20:28). The mystery of the cross lies within the will and the purpose and the design of God himself.

THE IMPERATIVES OF FAITH

We recall the imperatives that are laid upon the Christian believer who has been brought to saving faith in Christ. We have taken note of the principal questions that come into focus in our discussion of the statement of the Westminster Confession that "the principal acts of saving faith are, accepting, receiving, and resting upon Christ alone for justification, sanctification, and eternal life, by virtue of the covenant of grace."[4] A principal deduction to be drawn from all that has been said raises the question of what, in the light of the infinitely-valued redemption that Christ has achieved, is to be the life-structure and life-commitment of the believer.

That follows, we have seen, from the believer's consciousness that now, as a result of the grace of regeneration conveyed to him by the Holy Spirit, he is a new person in Christ Jesus. In adding briefly to our discussion of the imperatives of faith in a previous chapter, we raise at this point a preliminary caution regarding the Christian believer's standing and progress in sanctification. In that respect, a matter of concern arises on the level of human psychology.

Psychology as a secular discipline takes up questions of mind and behavior traits that attempt to explain human conduct and relations to social and cultural situations. We do not need any detailed discussion on those levels for our present purposes. When we speak of psychology, we are using the word in the sense that underlies a true biblical psychology. The word comes from the Greek root, "psyche," the first meaning of which is "soul." We are concerned, then, with certain aspects of the soul, particularly, in our present case, as the individual in his soulish aspect has been renewed by the grace of God in regeneration. The state of the

---

4. Westminster Confession of Faith, XIV:2. See the discussion in chapter 4 above.

soul as that refers to the individual person in his unregenerate condition, and the capacities of the faculties of the soul in that state, have been adequately explored in previous contexts. We move now to the regenerate state and reflect briefly on what has already been said.

Our proposition, in short, is that regeneration does not produce among Christians uniform psychological types. Within the church are to be found, or should be found, a variety of types of people, exhibiting variations of particular characteristics of personhood. What that means is that it is a serious mistake to imagine that members of the church should, or should be expected to, exhibit precisely the same personality characteristics, predilections, and preferences as everybody else in matters of less than critical doctrine. Regeneration does not produce "peas in a pod."

It is a mistake within the church to expect all people to react in the same way to given situations or to be made to feel that they must conform to stated norms which might, on careful consideration, amount to attempts to construct a new legalism, or that they should all be doing the same thing in the same way at the same time. Individual consciences are, under individual commitments to the law of God as set forth in the Scriptures, sacrosanct. It is a characteristic of the world that in spite of frequent protestations to the contrary, people generally attempt to attain conformity with peer groups or classes. Often, claims to individuality cloak a desire to be free simply to conform. Individuality of personhood is then lost and destroyed. Our proposition argues against any slavish wish or demand for conformity for its own sake within the church. Indeed, the grace of regeneration of which we have spoken gives to the Christian a new freedom, a new "liberty wherewith Christ hath made us free" (Gal 5:1). And individual expressions of that freedom, within, as has been said, honest subscription to the mandates of the law of God, are to be fully respected.

What has just been said is of critical importance. The freedom of individual expression and personhood exists within the Christian realization of the benefits of his new regenerate status. By regeneration, the faculties of the soul have been renewed as to their abilities and capacities. Of principal importance is the fact that by regenerating grace the harmony of the faculties has been restored and now again the mind resumes its place as the prince of the faculties of the soul. In the statement of the gospel it is important to understand that its first appeal is to the mind. Only the soul that is born again by the grace of regeneration can respond to the gospel, and that response comes to expression because the mind has been primarily engaged in assent to the truth of God that has been presented to it. That is so, at the same time as the affective and the volitional faculties, the heart and the will, have moved the individual in a whole-souled confession to the cross of Christ.

In the ongoing Christian life, then, the renewed and sanctified mind is to lead and direct the soul. That is why the apostle stated: "Be not conformed to this world: but be ye transformed by the renewing of your mind" (Rom 12:2). Two things follow. First, difficulties arise in the Christian life, and occasions of sin are entertained and disrupt the peace of the soul, because at the moment and for a time the Christian believer has ceased to think christianly. Second, what is now being said as to psychological differences among Christians is consistent with the individual's working out of the meaning and the application to his life of the revealed doctrines of the faith.

But within that context, it is a matter of clear observation that people by nature exhibit, and we can say are blessed with, widely different personality traits. Some are naturally effervescent, active, "on the go." Others are reflective, meditative, and more deliberative. Some individuals are naturally disposed to exhibit primarily emotional interpretations of situations and are readily given to empathy. Others are more pronouncedly cerebral in their interpretations and reactions. It is not necessary to attempt any exhaustive classification of psychological types. What is important to bear in mind is that if one is naturally an "outgoing" person before regeneration, he or she will tend to be an "outgoing" person after regeneration. If one is naturally meditative before regeneration, he or she will tend to be meditative after regeneration. In the light of that two things are to be said.

First, the grace of God, communicated in the first place in regeneration and then in the progress in sanctification, is not primarily designed to destroy and replace natural gifts, endowments, and abilities. Regeneration, to the contrary, is designed to take natural endowments and transform them into usefulness for service in the kingdom of Christ. That divine transformation of personal endowments expands also to the transformation, and to the sanctification for use in Christ's kingdom, of natural personality characteristics.

Second, full respect is therefore to be paid to the various ways in which different individuals, with, as has been said, different endowments of soul and different personhood characteristics, make up the unity of the body of Christ. To invoke the analogy of the body that the apostle used to good effect, not all Christians are hands, or feet, or heads. God has called into his church the various types of persons, from different backgrounds and different life trajectories, whom he has ordained to make up the body of the church. He has done that in such a way that the office and function of the church he has designed might be fully and harmoniously realized.

Observation forces the conclusion that church administrations have in some instances been at fault in the foregoing respects. Too ready tendencies to expect, even to call for and require, conformity in conduct, preferences, and behavior among church members have been apparent. The "peas in a pod" syndrome has been a disrupting, rather than cohesive, influence in the church. Recognition has not been granted to the necessary integration into the body of Christ of the diversity of personhood with which God has blessed his regenerate people.

Our point in making the foregoing observations is to suggest that careful distinctions need to be drawn, particularly, perhaps, but not exclusively, in the case of newer or younger Christians, between genuine occasions of sin and occasions simply of different personhood characteristics. We have seen in the preceding chapter that the cross of Christ is the refuge for sin, for sin in regenerate as well as unregenerate people. But it is our wish to avoid the imposition on individual Christians of any suggestion that mere differences of personality endowments do, in themselves, constitute sin or failure to live a full Christian life. The entire biblical doctrine of the church, and of the unity of the brethren within the church militant that God has ordained, points unmistakably in a different direction.

But the question persists: What are the imperatives of life with Christ that are laid upon the Christian believer? In our discussion of the believer's progressive sanctification we have seen that the residual propensity to sin that remains within him can and does give rise to actions and thoughts and imaginations that not only tarnish the holiness of life but, as the apostle stated it, "grieve . . . the holy Spirit of God, whereby ye are sealed unto the day of redemption" (Eph 4:30). Without undue repetition, we ask at this final point, what is it that is expected of the healthy

Christian life? The ethical directive and imperative is consistently drawn from the apostolic doctrinal arguments. In its negative expression it is seen as the necessity for the mortification of sin: "Mortify therefore your members which are upon the earth." (Col 3:5). In its positive aspect it is seen in the same apostle's statement to the Colossians: "As ye have therefore received Christ Jesus the Lord, so walk ye in him" (Col 2:6). We have already inspected the details. There will be progress in sanctification, we have said, as there is progress in the mortification of sin.

But the question presses on the Christian conscience: How is the walk with Christ to become reality in life? How is the mortification of sin to come to real effect in the Christian journey? The apostle has again stated the sure directive: "This I say then, *Walk in the Spirit*, and ye shall not fulfil the lust of the flesh" (Gal 5:16, italics added). And again: "If ye, *through the Spirit* do mortify the deeds of the body, ye shall live" (Rom 8:13, italics added). Against the residual propensity to sin that remains in the Christian, God has promised to give to his saints his Holy Spirit, that as they walk with him, in and by his enlightenment and guidance, the sinful frailties of the flesh and their influence are diminished. Our Lord had said during the supper on the night on which he was betrayed: "When he, the Spirit of truth, is come, he will guide you into all truth" (John 16:13). The guidance of the Holy Spirit who is there promised, and whom Christ sent in fulfillment of the promise when he ascended again to glory, guides his people, not only into truth in the cognitive sense of knowledge and awareness. He guides us also into the meaning of the way of life in the truth, into life and behavior patterns that are consistent with the truth. To those ends, God gives "the Holy Spirit to them that ask him" (Luke 11:13).

Finally, how, to recapitulate, have all the benefits of which we have spoken come about? Christ came, we have seen according to his own declaration, as the good shepherd to give his life for his sheep. "As a shepherd seeketh out his flock in the day that he is among his sheep that are scattered; so will I seek out my sheep, and will deliver them" (Ezek 34:12). In a wonderful anticipation of what we have seen as the flinging open of the invitation of the gospel to all the nations and peoples of the world, the prophet continues: "I will bring them out from the people, and gather them from the countries . . . I will feed them in a good pasture." In that remarkable prophetic promise God laid before his people of old the prospect of the coming of the Redeemer in fulfillment of all his redemptive designs. We see Christ the divine Redeemer in the figure of the servant David in the promise that "I will set up one shepherd over them, and he shall feed them, even my servant David . . . and he shall be their shepherd" (Exek 34:23).

The imperative that therefore presses on the Christian consciousness may be stated in the words of Peter that evince the uniformity of the apostolic testimony: "Gird up the loins of your mind, be sober, and hope to the end for the grace that is to be brought unto you at the revelation of Jesus Christ; As obedient children, not fashioning yourselves according to the former lusts in your ignorance: But as he which hath called you is holy, so be ye holy in all manner of conversation [or conduct]" (1 Pet 1:13–15).

THE JOY OF THE CHRISTIAN LIFE

As the Christian believer contemplates the imperatives laid upon him by reason of his redemption by the cross of Christ, he does so in the context of the realization that the Christian life is a life of joy. That realization stands against the blankness and the natural despair of life outside of Christ. That does not in any sense overlook the "slings and arrows" that life in the everyday inevitably encounters, or the assaults on one's Christian status and experience by the world, the flesh, and the devil. It is true that at the entrance to the Christian life there is a sorrow for sin that the Spirit of God in his awakening work breeds in the human consciousness. It is a sadness and remorse, the sorrow and the shame of sin, that drives a sinner to the cross of Christ. But the new life in Christ to which the sinner is introduced at the cross is a life of joy. It is a life grounded in the realization of the peace that the Spirit of God imparts to the sin-weary soul. The sinner knows that now, by virtue of the propitiatory offering of the Son of God, God is at peace with his people (Rom 5:1). The Christian life, lived out in holiness by the grace of the Spirit of God is, as the apostle Peter stated it, one of "joy unspeakable and full of glory" (1 Pet 1:8). The joy, the peace, the calmness of the Christian life come inevitably to expression because, as an old evangelical writer of the late-seventeenth-century put it, the Christian life is "the life of God in the soul of man."[5]

---

5. Scougal, *The Life of God in the Soul of Man*.

It is in no sense true, of course, nor is it to be expected, that the life of the redeemed saint in the world is a life of unbrokenly peaceful and joyful living out of his days. We have already looked at some aspects of the possibility and the fact of the Christian's falling again into sin. We have become all too clearly aware of the anguish and the torture of the temptation to sin. We have known that the peace and the joy and the calmness of contentment in Christ can be broken by the pressure of the "body of sin" (Rom 6:6), the weakness of the flesh, the subtlety of the adversary of our souls, and the discipline of the Spirit's dealing with us in the process of our sanctification. The Christian knows the possibility of the brokenness of his joy. But he knows, too, the meaning and effect of his repentant cry with the Psalmist: "Take not thy holy spirit from me. Restore unto me the joy of thy salvation" (Ps 51:11–12).

But with it all, we have said that the Christian life is a life of joy. For in all of its pressures and its failings, the cross of Christ is repeatedly and always its refuge and its haven from the storm. The Christian has known, by reason of the release from the burden of sin at the cross of Christ and from the ministry to him of the Holy Spirit whom Christ has sent (John 14:16, 26; 15:26; 16:13), the joy of his union with Christ. He knows, as a result, the assurance of eternal security and safety in the life that the Christ of the cross gives him. He knows, in the new self-awareness that comes in his embrace of life in Christ, that his status is now what it is because the cross of Christ has dealt with all his sin. That is the refuge of the saints in every attack against them by the devil and his angels. The devil must fail in every attempt to destroy the Christian's joy by the remembrance of sins that are past, for the cross of Christ declares that "there is therefore now no condemnation to them which are in Christ Jesus" (Rom 8:1).

The Savior of sinners, "despised and rejected of men; a man of sorrows, and acquainted with grief" (Isa 53:3) who had "no form nor comeliness . . . no beauty that we should desire him" (Isa 53:2), has become to the repentant sinner the "altogether lovely" one (Song 5:16). In that, the cross of Christ is the sinner's joy. In his consciousness rings the truth of the prophet's exclamation: "I will rejoice in the LORD, I will joy in the God of my salvation" (Hab 3:18). The cross of Christ introduces the sinner to all of the riches of the graces of Christ and to the promise of our Lord who has said: "Ask and ye shall receive, that your joy may be full" (John 16:24).

All of the benefits of the Christian life accrue to the redeemed sinner by virtue of his union with Christ. Our Lord has laid transparently bare the reality of that union in his high priestly prayer for his saints: "Holy Father . . . I pray . . . that they all may be one; as thou, Father, art in me, and I in thee, that they also may be one in us" (John 17:11, 21). We have taken note of Berkhof's summary of the reality of the union: "The initial act is that of Christ, who unites believers to himself *by regenerating them* and thus producing faith in them. On the other hand, the believer also unites himself to Christ by a conscious act of faith, and continues the union, under the influence of the Holy Spirit, by the constant exercise of faith."[6] The vital, spiritual, and indissoluble union with Christ propels our thought, our worship, and our praise to the highest level of the meaning of redemptive realities that Christ has established for us. The life of Christ, by his Spirit, courses through the being and the life of those whom he has redeemed and brought to himself. On those grounds the apostle exclaimed: "I am crucified with Christ: nevertheless I live; yet not I, but Christ liveth in me" (Gal 2:20).

The joy of the Christian life turns on the invitations of Christ that in themselves have credence and virtue by reason of the work of salvation that he wrought on the cross. He has said to weary, sin-laden souls: "Come unto me . . . and I will give you rest" (Matt 11:28). And he says, patiently and continually, to those he redeemed: "I stand at the door, and knock: if any man open the door, I will come in to him, and will sup with him, and he with me" (Rev 3:20). In that direction lies the Christian's *summum bonum*, his highest good, the possibility of the company, comfort, and companionship of Christ who has saved him and the realization of the benefits of the riches of his grace. It is the height of Christian wisdom to entertain the company of the Savior who thereby calls to his people to convey to them his sanctifying grace. May God grant that it may be so.

---

6. Berkhof, *Systematic Theology*, 450, italics added.

7

Biblical Inspiration and Authority

As we anticipated at the beginning, we return in this final chapter to a question that lies at the foundation of all that has been said to this point. Our objective is to explore somewhat more fully the basis of the claims in the preceding chapters that the Scriptures are the inspired Word of God and the only reliable source of truth. They provide the ground on which we stand in the search for meaning. Those claims derive from the fact that the Holy Spirit of God is the primary or the ultimate author of the scriptural text in the original autographs, and that definable relations, though not equal ultimacy, exist between the Holy Spirit and the secondary human authors. By reason of God's providential preservation of the Scriptures and by virtue of proper translation, we have at this time the inerrant Word of God. An important contribution to the doctrine of Scripture exists in what has been seen as the parallel, or the analogy, between the divine and the human natures of Christ and the divine and human elements of Scripture. The comments on that aspect contained in the following will be expanded briefly to take note of some problem issues that arise from contemporary discussions on that level.

The Scriptures, we have concluded, provide the only adequate explanation of the human condition. The assumption we hold as determinative is that, as Cornelius Van Til has put it expressively: "The Bible . . . [is] authoritative on everything of which it speaks. And it *speaks of everything*."[1] By that we mean that it speaks of everything either directly or indirectly. Van Til continues: "It tells us not only of the Christ and his work but it also tells us who God is and whence the universe has come. It gives us a philosophy of history as well as history. Moreover, the information on these subjects is woven into an inextricable whole. It is only if you reject the

---

1. Van Til, *Defense of the Faith*, 8.

Bible as the word of God that you can separate its so-called religious and moral instruction from what it says, e.g., about the physical universe."[2]

It is not possible at this point to address in any fullness the historic development of the doctrine of Scripture.[3] But the following comments will confirm that in the Scriptures the meaning and message of the cross are copiously and eloquently addressed.

SOME PRELIMINARY CONSIDERATIONS

First, the Scripture is only indirectly the first principle of knowledge. The Reformed theological tradition has referred to the first principle of theology, the *principium essendi* or the essential foundation, as the fact that "all of our knowledge of God has its origin in God himself."[4] God is the *principium essendi*, of theology. The question follows of the means by which God's knowledge, or the knowledge that God requires us to have of him, is conveyed to us. The Scriptures, then, provide the *principium cognoscendi* of theology, or the true and reliable source of knowledge. Or more precisely, we refer to the Scriptures as the *principium cognoscendi externum*, the objective source of knowledge, and to the faith that God gives us, and whereby we believe, as the *principium cognoscendi internum* or the subjective source or instrument of knowledge.[5] As God is "infinite, eternal, and unchangeable in his being. . . and truth,"[6] he can and does speak only truth, and for that reason we hold to the infallibility and inerrancy of what we shall see he has said in the Scriptures.

Second, our approach to the doctrine of Scripture is therefore determined by what we hold as our basic apologetic presupposition. That is the presupposition that *God is*. God does not exist at the end of a logical syllogism structured by autonomous human thought. God is not knowable because we have conjured God or reached him by an evidential-

---

2. Idem.

3. For classic discussions see Calvin, *Institutes*, vol. 1, 69–228; Turretin, *Institutes*, vol. 1, 55–167; Bavinck, *Reformed Dogmatics*, vol. 1, 283–494; Kuyper, *Sacred Theology*, 397–563; Kuyper, *Work of the Holy Spirit*, 56–92; Warfield, *Inspiration and Authority*; Young, *Thy Word is Truth*; Murray, "The Attestation of Scripture"; Murray, "The Holy Scriptures"; Murray, *Calvin on Scripture*.

4. Berkhof, *Systematic Theology*, New Edition, *Introductory Volume*, 95. See Muller, *Post-Reformation Reformed Dogmatics*, vol. 2, 149–223.

5. This and some parts of the following paragraphs in this section are dependent on Vickers, *Christian Confession*, chap. 4, "The Necessity and Canonicity of Scripture."

6. Westminster Shorter Catechism, Question 4.

inductive process of reasoning. God is knowable and known because he has revealed himself. The chain of disclosure runs from God to man, not from man to God. God is known because he has spoken, because in real time and real history he has made a self-disclosure. Meaning resides, not in what we ask about God or imagine we can discover about God, but in what God has said to us. God exists and has made a revelation to us, and because we see *that* in the Scriptures they convey to us the authority to which we refer. We know that the Scriptures are the Word of God because in them we hear the voice of God speaking. In that, we shall see, the Scriptures attest their own scripturicity.

Third, from what has been said two implications follow. First, it is only as God has taken the initiative and revealed himself that knowledge is possible. Knowledge is possible for us because, as to our knowledge and as to our being, we are the analogue of God. Because by creation we have been established as the image of God we are necessarily open to God's communication to us. We stand inevitably and inescapably before the face of God. "In him we live, and move, and have our being" (Acts 17:28). Second, that in turn determines the fact and the necessity of God's revelation as that is conveyed to us in the Scriptures.

Fourth, we say more particularly that the necessity of God's *revelation* follows from the *finitude* in which we were created. We hold in all our theological formulation to the Creator-creature distinction. While the necessity of *revelation* follows from our *finitude*, the necessity of *inscripturated revelation* and the content of it follows from our *sin*. The Scripture became necessary because of the possibility of natural defilement, by reason of sin, of oral transmission of the dicta of God. That proposition leaves aside the question whether, if Adam had not sinned, there might have been an inscripturation of God's word to man. We do not know in detail what Adam's life might have been if he had not fallen, and to address that question at length is to fall beyond the Scriptures into idle speculation; we know only that Adam would in due time have been elevated to eternal life, confirmed in moral status, and his nature changed accordingly. What is being said is that the necessity of *inscripturation* follows from our sin (as distinct from the necessity of revelation as such that follows from our finitude) because Adam *did* sin, and God's grace from that point on is directed to the redemption of the elect who descended from Adam.

Fifth, along with our basic apologetic presupposition that *God is*, we hold to a fundamental hermeneutical principle, or principle of interpretation. In his speech to man God has revealed his own thoughts (of which, as has been said, by reason of our finitude we may possess a knowledge analogically), and he has made known to us his purposes with relation to the reality that he spoke into existence. God has disclosed those purposes, including his purposes of redemption, in covenantal form. Our hermeneutical principle, therefore, is that the meaning of God's stated covenant determines the manner in which we hear the Scriptures speak. That principle and our apologetic presupposition that *God is* are correlative in their impact and effects. It follows that God's revelation is to be understood as a covenantal revelation, and the inscripturation of revelation as a covenantal inscripturation.

By the statement that we must understand God's inscripturation of his Word as a covenantal inscripturation, the following is intended. As all reality external to the Godhead is covenantally structured, as man himself is a covenant creature, as all of God's dealings with man whom he created in his image are to be seen and understood in terms of covenantal fulfillment, as the eternal glory of God to which creation and the redeemed host of God move is the grand objective of what God has covenantally decreed, so all of God's actions in the course of history are aspects of his sovereign covenantal realizations. Those actions include, as we are now discussing it, the inscripturation of his Word. We observed at an earlier point that similarly, the incarnation of the Second Person of the Godhead is to be understood as a covenantal incarnation. The implication follows, as will be discussed at length, that both the union of the divine and human natures in the Person of our Lord and the divine and human character of the Scriptures are aspects of God's fulfillment of what was necessary for the realization of the objectives of the Covenant of Redemption. As Douglas Kelly has observed at the beginning of his recent *Systematic Theology*, "God reveals Himself . . . by means of His Word and Spirit personally within the context of the covenant community."[7]

Sixth, it follows that in the speech of God in the Scriptures he has made an anthropomorphic communication to us. That is to say, "God reveals himself to man according to man's ability to receive his revela-

---

7. Kelly, *Systematic Theology*, 13.

tion. *All revelation is anthropomorphic.*"[8] God has condescended to speak to us in the language of men. Calvin comments on Ezekiel 9:3–4: "God cannot be comprehended by us, unless as far as he accommodates himself to our standard. . . . God is incomprehensible in himself"; and on 1 Corinthians 2:7, Calvin comments that "God . . . accommodates himself to our capacity in addressing us."[9]

THE SCRIPTURAL DOCTRINE OF SCRIPTURE

We shall return below to the important fact that as to the composition of the Scriptures a distinction is to be made between the primary or ultimate and the secondary authors. The words of Scripture are the words of the Holy Spirit. But clearly, every book of the Bible has a human author. That in no sense means, however, that the Scriptures bear the mark of human fallibility and that error must therefore be contained in the Bible. In short, by reason that the Holy Spirit is the divine author of the Bible, and by reason of the fact that it cannot be said that the primary and the secondary authors are equally ultimate, the possibility of error in the original manuscripts does not exist. That fact will provide an entry to what has become a matter of principal debate at the present time, having to do with the so-called incarnational understanding of Scripture. Abraham Kuyper, for example, concludes that an analogy exists between the sinlessness of the incarnate Christ and the fact that the Scriptures are without error. But our immediate concern is with the testimony the Scriptures bear to their own scripturicity.[10] And that establishes the absence of error in the light of secondary human authorship. In other words, the Scripture claims inerrancy for itself. Murray observes that "the basis of faith in the Bible is the witness the Bible itself bears to the fact that it is God's Word . . . The doctrine of Scripture must be elicited from the Scripture just as any other doctrine should be."[11]

In support of that conclusion Murray advances several arguments, some of which can be noted briefly. First, the Scriptures do not bear any

---

8. Van Til, *Christian Theory of Knowledge*, 37. See also the extensive discussion in Bahnsen, *Van Til's Apologetics*, chap. 4.

9. Calvin, *Commentaries*, loc. cit.

10. An early but very valuable discussion is contained in Packer, *'Fundamentalism'*, chap. 4.

11. Murray, "The Attestation of Scripture," 7–8.

negative evidence. "Scripture does not adversely criticize itself."[12] That is to say, a unity and a harmony exist between the several parts of Scripture. Second, as to positive evidence, the Scriptures repeatedly introduce the words of the prophets with the assertion, "thus saith the Lord," thereby claiming for themselves divine origin and authority. Third, it is noted that at John 10:30 Christ asserted his deity in the statement that "I and my Father are one," and by adducing a brief statement from Psalm 82:6 he rebutted the cavil of the Jews that he had spoken blasphemy. In pivoting his defense on that Old Testament text, our Lord indicated that he considered the Scriptures as unassailably definitive and trustworthy. For as he went on to say, "the Scripture cannot be broken" (John 10:35). He thereby "expresses . . . his own view of the inviolability of Scripture."[13] Fourth, the self-attestation of the Scriptures is evident again in the reflection of the apostle Paul who, in reference to the Old Testament text, stated that "whatsoever things were written aforetime were written for our learning, that we through patience and comfort of the scriptures might have hope" (Rom 15:4). And again, in the context preceding the apostle's conclusion that "all scripture is given by inspiration of God" (2 Tim 3:16), he referred to the "holy scriptures" that Timothy had known from his childhood, Scriptures which, Paul said, "are able to make thee wise unto salvation through faith which is in Christ Jesus" (2 Tim 3:15). What is thereby being said is that "the organic unity of both Testaments is the presupposition of the appeal to the authority of the Old Testament and of allusion to it in which the New Testament abounds."[14]

It can be added that the Scriptures' claim to their own scripturicity is confirmed by the progressive manner in which the revelation of God's covenantal purposes is contained in them. There is noticeably and beyond doubt a progressive development of scriptural revelation, while there is not, of course, any progressive development of God's eternally declared plan and purpose. It is beyond our present scope to trace the manner in which, in the Old Testament witness, the terms of that covenant are unfolded and the progressive implementation of it is realized, through the patriarchs, Abraham, Moses, David, and the pre- and post-exilic prophets. But for the devout enquirer there lies on the very surface of the text an inescapable unity and harmony in the revelation.

12. Ibid., 10–11.
13. Ibid., 25.
14. Ibid., 33.

That covenantal disclosure continues to the "new covenant" that was foreseen by the prophet Jeremiah (Jer 31:31–34), and the consistency of the prophecy and fulfillment is established by the conjunction of Joel 2:28–32 and Acts 2:16–18. There we have the promise and the fulfillment of the coming of the Holy Spirit to the church in a new fullness, a crowning aspect of the realization of the "new covenant" in Christ that Jeremiah had foreseen.

It is an aspect of the Scriptures' self-attestation that the apostle Paul regarded his own words as carrying divine sanction and authority. At 1 Corinthians 14:37 he claimed that "the things that I write unto you are the commandments of the Lord." At 1 Corinthians 2:10 he referred to things that "God hath revealed unto us by his Spirit."

The post-Reformation confessions have observed with reference to the Scriptures: "Our full persuasion and assurance of the infallible truth, and divine authority thereof, is from the inward work of the Holy Spirit, bearing witness by and with the word in our hearts."[15] Much has accordingly been made in this connection of the "internal testimony of the Spirit." But the nature of the reality involved has not always been clearly understood. In the neo-orthodoxy that was current in the early part of the last century the claim was advanced on similar lines that the Bible was not in itself the Word of God, but that it *became* the Word of God to the reader by reason of the witness it bore *to* the Word of God. In that, we have assumptions of subjective human consciousness supplanting the objectively given Word of God as the source and canon of belief. Developments of that kind have reappeared in the subsequent history of the church. For example, in the existential theology of the early twentieth century the saving relation that an individual might sustain to Christ was deemed to turn on what was referred to as an existential encounter with him, to the neglect of the scriptural call for repentance and faith in Christ who is our only redeemer. Similarly, the New Perspective on Paul theology of recent times, in the hands, particularly, of its influential proponent, N.T. Wright, as we saw in an earlier context, claims that "'the gospel' is not an account of how people get saved.... 'The gospel' is the announcement of Jesus' lordship ... [and] all those who have this faith [in Jesus' lordship] belong as full members of this family [the family of Abraham now redefined around Jesus Christ], on this basis and no other"[16]

---

15. Westminster Confession of Faith, I:5.
16. Wright, *What Saint Paul Really Said*, 133.

What is being said in such claims is that those are justified, and they are thereby reckoned to be within the kingdom of God, who declare that Jesus is Lord. The gospel of justification by faith in Christ as Savior is again replaced by a subjectively generated statement of concurrence with Christ's lordship. That concurrence is reckoned to be provoked by hearing the declaration of the lordship of Christ, but how that conviction is brought about is not made clear. The flattening of justification to such a mere statement of belief in Christ's lordship, with the rejection it carries with it of the imputation to the sinner of Christ's forensic righteousness, once again replaces the objectivity of the Scriptures as the Word of God with a not-very-well-defined human subjectivity.

To all such claims we respond, on the ground of arguments we have already adduced, that the Bible is fully and objectively the Word of God, inherently and qualitatively, and that its authority in no sense depends, and cannot be conceived to depend, on any subjective human construction of what it says. That that is so is clearly confirmed by the very fact that the Bible is unrelenting in disclosing and insisting on the natural depravity of the human mind and the entailment of sin into which all mankind had fallen as a result of Adam's dereliction. It is the "internal testimony of the Spirit" that remedies that natural incapacity and enables the truth of the Scriptures' own attestation to be seen.

But two things are to be said in that connection. First, the internal testimony of the Spirit is not to be construed as a bare testimony or a telling to the individual person that the Bible is the Word of God. On the contrary, the internal testimony is the work of the Holy Spirit in so informing the mind that the darkness of blindness is taken away and the individual is now able to see what was always there to be seen but was obscured by the enslavement to the god of this world that the natural state of sin involved. The internal testimony of the Spirit, Murray has observed, "is regeneration on the noetic side [an opening of the mind] because it is regeneration coming to its expression in our understanding in the response of the renewed mind to the evidence Scripture contains of its divine character."[17] John Owen made the point in characteristic seventeenth-century language: "There is an especial work of the Spirit of God on the minds of men, communicating spiritual wisdom, light, and understanding unto them, necessary unto their discerning and apprehending aright the mind of God in his word, and the understanding

---

17. Murray, "The Attestation of Scripture," 49.

of the mysteries of heavenly truth contained therein."[18] In anticipation of what we shall refer to as the divine ordination of the *form* as well as the *content* of Scripture, Bavinck has brought together those joint considerations in his response to the question of the internal testimony of the Spirit. That witness of the Spirit "comes to us indirectly in all the divine characteristics (criteria, marks) which are imprinted on the *content and form* of Scripture. It also comes to us directly in all those positive pronouncements Scripture contains with respect to its divine origin."[19]

Abraham Kuyper addressed a similar question in his running debates with what were referred to in his time as the Ethical theologians. In the course of a discussion of "Apostolic Inspiration," Kuyper observed that the Ethical theologians effectively maintained that inspiration was simply a peculiarly high degree of the illumination that had been received in the grace of regeneration.[20] But the Reformed doctrine is very much to the contrary. The apostles were the recipients and custodians of a special, objective revelation that carried with it the unique inspiration of the Holy Spirit. As has been said, the words they wrote were the words of the Holy Spirit. As Kuyper concludes: "The unique position and extraordinary power of the apostles . . . was granted to them alone and to no one else."[21] The inspiration of which they were the beneficiaries for purposes of the discharge of their unique office and function was in no sense to be confused with a mere elevation of the grace of regeneration.

THE FORM AND AUTHORSHIP OF SCRIPTURE

Against the foregoing statements two questions deserve more precise notice. First, what is to be said of the relation between, on the one hand, the fact of both the primary or ultimate and the secondary authorship of the Scriptures and, on the other hand, the *form* in which the Scriptures have been given? And second, what is to be said of the modern (in fact,

---

18. Owen, *Works*, vol. 3, 124–25.

19. Bavinck, *Reformed Dogmatics*, vol. 1, 597, italics added. For an extended discussion of Calvin's doctrine of the internal testimony of the Spirit see Warfield, "Calvin's Doctrine of the Knowledge of God," 70–130, reprinted in Warfield, *Calvin and Calvinism*, 70–130.

20. Kuyper, *Work of the Holy Spirit*, 153. See also Gaffin, *God's Word in Servant-Form*, 30. I am indebted to Gaffin's work for directing me to the importance of the place occupied by Kuyper and Bavinck in the history of the doctrine of Scripture.

21. Kuyper, *Work of the Holy Spirit*, 155.

the not entirely modern) claim that importance attaches to what we shall see as the analogy between the phenomenon of Scripture and the incarnation of our Lord? We shall take the first question first.

The question at issue concerns the extent to which, while it might be agreed that the Holy Spirit was in a unique way influential in the production of Scripture, the precise formation of the words of Scripture and the formation of the finished product were nevertheless the work of the human authors. When we refer to the *form* of Scripture we have in mind both the actual format of a specific human writer's presentation and the structure of the biblical corpus as a whole, as it presents a complete and unified statement of the revelation that God has chosen to make.[22] Our conclusion will be that the *form* of the Scriptures is a divine design and ordination, that it was designed and ordered as part of the divine intention before the foundation of the world, and that it is in no sense attributable to the organizational skill and originality of autonomous human authors. That is clear from the fact that the Scripture is *God's* Word and that in designing and giving it he has done all things according to the counsel of his will (Eph 1:11).

We may observe Kuyper's claim of a "predestined Bible," which, he says, "was spoken of in Reformed circles, by which was understood that the *preconceived form* of the Holy Scriptures had been given already from eternity in the counsel of God."[23] More particularly, as to the formation of the Scriptures:

> According to a plan, known to God alone, a structure is gradually raised on which . . . different persons have labored without agreement, and without having seen the whole. . . . Thus the plan of the Holy Scriptures was hidden, back of human consciousness, in the consciousness of God, and He it is, who in His time has so created each of these writers, so endowed, led and impelled them, that they have contributed what He wanted, and what after His plan and direction was to constitute His Scripture. The *conception*, therefore, has not gone out of men, but out of God," and the result was "of such a *content* and in such a *form*, as had been aimed at and willed by God.[24]

---

22. See Gaffin, *God's Word in Servant-Form* for a valuable discussion of related issues in the course of a rebuttal of certain conclusions of Rogers and McKim in their *Authority and Interpretation of the Bible*.

23. Kuyper, *Sacred Theology*, 474.

24. Ibid., 475.

In those claims Kuyper is fully in line with the seventeenth-century dogmatics. Owen, for example, observes that "the Holy Spirit of God hath *prepared and disposed of* the Scripture so as it might be a most sufficient and absolutely perfect way and means of communicating unto our minds that saving knowledge of God and his will which is needful that we may live unto him, and come unto the enjoyment of him in his glory."[25]

The fact that the Bible has come to us in a preconceived form warrants the conclusion, as we have already observed, that the inscripturation of God's revelation is a *covenantal* inscripturation. Our doctrine of the Scriptures falls far below what is worthy of their own attestation if we do not see and maintain that, as is the case with all other aspects of God's salvific intentions, the giving of the Scriptures is again a covenantal fulfillment. God has said what he has said, and he has said it in the form he has, as part of his overarching covenantal purpose of ordering all things, including notably the salvation of his elect, for his own eternal glory. When we see that the Scriptures thus assume their place in the divinely ordered fulfillment of God's salvific covenant, the dual questions of the necessity and the authority of the Scriptures are clearly resolved. For first, the inscripturation of God's purposes in salvation and the *modus operandi* of it underline starkly the *necessity* of the Scriptures. The Scriptures became necessary by reason of our sin, and in them God has accommodated his speech to our perilous condition. It follows, then, that the *authority* of Scripture is suspended on its *necessity*. God in his wisdom and grace having deemed the Scriptures necessary for the reason stated, they immediately assume the status of authoritative. The Scripture is authoritative, that is, firstly because it contains the speech of God, and secondly because in it God has said all that he has to say to man in his state of sin. There is no other word from God. The Scriptures alone are his definitive and final word to us. There is therefore no other authority that can or does provide both an entrance to meaning on all levels of reality, knowledge, and existence and, in particular, the understanding of what it is that the sovereign God, redeemer and judge, requires of us.

When we have said that the *form* as well as the *content* of the Scriptures is due to the sovereign ordering of the Holy Spirit, it is not necessary for our present purposes to labor the fact that the human authors were in every relevant respect providentially prepared by God

---

25. Owen, *Works*, vol. 4, 187, italics added.

himself for the work they were destined to do. It is necessary, of course, as Edward J. Young has put it in his very valuable *Thy Word is Truth*, "to do full justice to what the Bible has to say about its human side."[26] Suffice it to say that God providentially prepared the human authors, in their personal histories, endowments, temperaments, and developments of learning, culture, and maturity of mind for the task to which he called them. We can say with Young at that point that "very wondrous was God's providential preparation and equipment of those men whom He had appointed to be the human instruments in the writing of Scripture. Thus He prepared and raised up an Isaiah, a Jeremiah, a John, and a Paul. His work of providence and His special work of inspiration should be regarded as complementing one another."[27] That being so, we have already said that the very words of the Scripture are the words of God, implying that by reason of the superintending influence of the Holy Spirit, the human authors, with their own particular levels of learning, style, personality, temperament, and source availabilities, consistently wrote what God intended to be written. Given, as Bavinck maintains, his so-called "organic view of revelation and inspiration . . . ordinary human life and natural life . . . is also made serviceable to the thoughts of God."[28]

Kuyper refers to "the secondary authors" as "amanuenses of the Holy Spirit."[29] But from what has been said it is clear that that can in no sense be taken to imply that the human authors were mere mindless automata. To say that they were, and that they were simply the recipients of dictation, as some critics have argued, is a parody and misrepresentation of the scriptural doctrine of Scripture. Calvin, it is true, as Young notes, states in his comment on 2 Timothy 3:16 that "whoever then wishes to profit in the Scriptures, let him, first of all, lay down this as a settled point, that the Law and the Prophets are not a doctrine delivered according to the will and pleasure of men but *dictated* by the Holy Spirit."[30] But it is clear from Calvin's fuller argument that by his use of the word "dictated" he intends to speak consistently with the thought of the Bible

---

26. Young, *Thy Word is Truth*, 65.
27. Ibid., 70.
28. Bavinck, *Reformed Dogmatics*, vol. 1, 443.
29. Kuyper, *Sacred Theology*, 480.
30. Calvin, *Commentaries*, loc. cit., italics added. See the fuller discussion in Young, op. cit., 65–82.

itself and to accord divine origin to the words of the Bible. He does not mean "dictation" in its modern connotation.

In what we have seen as the importance of keeping clear the relation between the primary or ultimate and the secondary authors of Scripture, Bavinck is one with his near-contemporary Kuyper. Bavinck rejects decisively a "mechanical notion of revelation [which] one-sidedly emphasizes the new, the supernatural element that is present in inspiration... This detaches the Bible writers from their personality, as it were, and lifts them out of the history of their time.... It allows them to function only as mindless, inanimate instruments in the hand of the Holy Spirit."[31] "God... treats human beings, not as blocks of wood, but as intelligent and moral beings."[32] And again, in summarizing his view of "organic inspiration," Bavinck captures the relevance and importance of what we have already drawn attention to as the divine ordination of the *form* as well as the *content* of Scripture when he says: "Scripture is the word of God; it not only contains but *is* the word of God.... *Form* and *content* interpenetrate each other and are inseparable."[33] In the Scriptures, "the human has become an instrument of the divine; the natural has become a revelation of the supernatural; the visible has become a sign and seal of the invisible."[34] In referring to the church fathers, some of whose comments might be thought to point in other directions, such as their "comparing the prophets and apostles, in the process of writing, with a cither, a lyre, a flute, or a pen in the hand of the Holy Spirit," Bavinck is quick to conclude that "in using these similes they only wanted to indicate that the Bible writers were the secondary authors and that God was the primary author."[35] The distinction in view has been well preserved, of course, in the subsequent history, in the English language writers such as Warfield, Murray, and Young, for example, as referred to in footnote 3 above. In that connection it is instructive to compare the Dutch consolidation of the Reformed doctrine of the inspiration of Scripture, in Kuyper and Bavinck,

---

31. Bavinck, *Reformed Dogmatics*, vol. 1, 431.
32. Ibid., 432.
33. Ibid., 443, italics added.
34. Idem.
35. Ibid., 431. For comment on Bavinck's position see Gaffin, *God's Word in Servant Form*, 72–76.

for example,[36] with that of the English language writers referred to.[37] An expanded discussion of the post-Reformation history of the doctrine of Scripture has been provided also by Richard Muller.[38]

INSPIRATION AND INCARNATION

An important contribution to our understanding of the doctrine of Scripture is contained in the claims of several theologians that an analogy exists between inscripturation (inspiration) and the incarnation of Christ. The question has come pointedly to issue in recent times and has raised a good deal of disturbed debate as a result of the work of Peter Enns. That is due principally to his *Inspiration and Incarnation: Evangelicals and the Problem of the Old Testament*, which has been seen as undermining the scriptural doctrine we have so far adduced.[39] But the question of whether a parallel exists between inspiration and incarnation has a longer history. Kuyper and Bavinck addressed the question at some length, and J.I. Packer drew attention to it in his *'Fundamentalism' and the Word of God*. It is worth taking brief note of Packer's analysis.

The problem Packer identifies is that certain critics had accused the evangelicals of falling prey to the false doctrine of Monophysitism, which argued that Christ had only one nature and denied the true humanity of our Lord.[40] Evangelicalism, it was claimed, to the extent that it maintained that same focus, tended to lose sight of the fact that Christ was truly man, and it failed also, as a result, to do justice to the human character of the Bible. If, that is to say, Christ was of only one nature, and that a divine nature, then by analogy it could be thought that the Bible also was only divine, to the neglect, as a result, of its human character and nature. The critics therefore thought their position to be superior in that it had regard to both the human and the divine natures in Christ and, analogously, to both the divine and human character of the Bible.

---

36. See Kuyper, *Sacred Theology*, 405–41, and Bavinck, *Reformed* Dogmatics, vol. 1, 387–448.

37. See Warfield, *Inspiration and Authority*, 105–226, and Young, op. cit., 85–109.

38. Muller, *Post-Reformation Reformed Dogmatics*, vol. 2.

39. Enns, *Inspiration and Incarnation*. For a fuller discussion of Enns' work see the review article by Waltke, "Revisiting *Inspiration and Incarnation*, " and Enns' rejoinder in the same issue of the *Westminster Theological Journal*; Waltke, "Interaction with Peter Enns"; Scott, "Inspiration and Interpretation of God's Word: Parts I and II."

40. Packer, *'Fundamentalism'*, 82.

Packer takes note of Gabriel Hebert's citation of R.H. Fuller to the effect that "we have to discern the treasure in earthen vessels: the divinity in Christ's humanity ... the Word of God in the fallible words of men."[41] We shall see that there is a sense in which the christological parallel does exist and is legitimate, but the critical claim to which we have just referred falls, of course, by reason of its reference to the "fallible" words of men.

Packer is himself cautious about embracing the parallel and finds that the analogy "can be only a limited one."[42] He agrees that "human as well as divine qualities are to be recognized in Scripture ... [and] we do in fact recognize the reality of both."[43] But he wishes to state carefully the meaning of whatever analogy is properly involved. In doing so, he puts his finger on the vitally necessary elements of the parallelism: "As our Lord, though truly man, was truly free from sin, so Scripture, though a truly human product, is truly free from error."[44] The error of the critics who had also adduced a parallel between Scripture and the incarnation was that it followed from their claim that as there were errors in the Bible so also Christ, as man, had erred and thereby sinned.

Benjamin Warfield makes a very necessary point in establishing a true and sustainable analogy between the Scriptures and the incarnation of Christ:

> As, in the case of Our Lord's person, the human nature remains truly human while yet it can never fall into sin or error because it can never act out of relation with the Divine nature into conjunction with which it has been brought; so in the case of the production of Scripture by the conjoint action of human and Divine factors, the human factors have acted as human factors, and have left their mark on the product as such, and yet cannot have fallen into that error which we say it is human to fall into, because they have not acted apart from the Divine factors, by themselves, but only under their unerring guidance.[45]

Warfield had cautioned us in the same context as to the sense in which, finally, we should hold to the inscripturation-incarnation analogy:

---

41. Packer, idem; Hebert, *Fundamentalism*, 78.
42. Packer, 'Fundamentalism', 83.
43. Idem.
44. Idem.
45. Warfield, *Inspiration and Authority*, 162–63.

> It has been customary... to speak of the Scriptures, because thus 'inspired,' as a Divine-human book, and to appeal to the analogy of Our Lord's Divine-human personality to explain their peculiar qualities as such.... But the analogy with Our Lord's Divine-human personality [where there was a hypostatic union, a union in his one divine personhood of the divine and human natures] may easily be pressed beyond reason. There is no hypostatic union between the Divine and the human in Scripture.[46]

We can say, however, that though there is no hypostatic union in inscripturation, a correspondence or parallel exists between inscripturation and incarnation in the following respect. In Reformed christology, following Chalcedon, the divine nature of our Lord is the *essential* locus of personality and the human nature is *contingent*, dependent on the divine, yet real in itself. Similarly, in Scripture, the divine, the authorship of God the Holy Spirit, is *essential*, and the human, the secondary authorship, is *contingent*, yet again in itself real.

Two further issues arise from Warfield's comments. First, the brief review we have given establishes that in the mainstream of Reformed theology a *parallel* or an *analogical relation* between inscripturation (inspiration) and the incarnation has been understood to exist. But second, it is necessary to understand more clearly *why*, or the *grounds on which*, that parallel is doctrinally meaningful.

The issue turns on what we have already argued as the *necessity* of God's revelation, grounded as that is not only in our finitude, but, in the instance of inscripturation, in our sin. We can bring that into conjunction with our previous remarks on the divine origin not only of the *content* of Scripture but also of its *form*. Consider the manner in which the writer to the Hebrews made the point: "God, who at sundry times and in divers manners spake in time past unto the fathers by the prophets, Hath in these last days spoken unto us by his Son" (Heb 1:1-2). Our focus is on the Word of God, the Logos, who has communicated to us in those various forms. Kuyper grasped the relation that is now involved:

> If man is created after the Image of God, and thus disposed to communion with the Eternal, then this *Word of God* also must be able to be grasped by man; and even after his fall into sin, this Word of God must go out to him, though now in a way suited to his condition. This takes place now, since man has received *being*

---

46. Ibid., 162.

and *consciousness*, in two ways. In the way of the *esse* [or being] by the *incarnation* of the Logos, and in the way of consciousness as *this selfsame Logos* becomes embodied in the Scripture. Both are the spoken Word; but in one case it is the Word 'become flesh,' in the other 'written,' and these two cover each other. Christ is the whole Scripture, and the Scripture brings the *esse* of the Christ to our consciousness.[47]

The analogy, or the parallel, between the Scripture (inspiration) and the incarnation exists, then, and is doctrinally sustainable by reason that in both, in their respective ways, we have the revelation of the divine Logos, the Word of God. Here, then, "the parallel maintains itself between the incarnate and the written Logos. As in the Mediator the Divine nature weds itself to the human, and appears before us in *its* form and figure, so also the Divine factor of the Holy Scripture clothes itself in the garment of our form of thought, and holds itself to our human reality."[48] "It is the one *Logos* which in Christ by incarnation, and in the Scripture by inscripturation goes out to humanity at large,"[49] and "from this special principium in God the saving power is extended centrally to our race, both by the ways of *being* and of *thought*, by incarnation and inspiration."[50]

Bavinck similarly concludes:

> The revelation that thus comes to us objectively from the side of God is to be differentiated into a general and special one.... Special revelation... is that conscious and free act of God by which he, in the way of a historical complex of special means (theophany, prophecy, miracle) that are concentrated in the person of Christ, makes himself known... to those human beings who live in the light of this special revelation... Both this general and this special revelation are primarily objective; and included in this objective special revelation, accordingly, is the revelation that occurs in the consciousness of prophets and apostles by addressive and interior speech, by divine inspiration in the sense of 2 Timothy 3:16.[51]

And again the correlation between incarnation and inscripturation is decisively established: "Inasmuch as in his person and work Christ

---

47. Kuyper, *Sacred Theology*, 476–77, italics partially added.
48. Ibid., 478.
49. Ibid., 401.
50. Ibid., 425.
51. Bavinck, *Reformed Dogmatics*, vol. 1, 350.

fully revealed the Father to us, that revelation is fully described for us in Scripture. . . . In Christ God both fully revealed and fully gave himself. Consequently also Scripture is complete; it is the perfected Word of God."[52] But it quite properly follows for Bavinck that "the incarnation of Christ demands that we trace it down into the depths of its humiliation, in all its weakness and contempt. The recording of the word, of revelation, invites us to recognize that dimension of weakness and lowliness, the servant form, also in Scripture. But just as Christ's human nature, however weak and lowly, remained free from sin, so also Scripture is 'conceived without defect or stain'; totally human in all its parts but also divine in all its parts."[53]

It would repeat our earlier argument to observe at length that the divine origin of the Scriptures in the manner just referred to establishes its necessity, authority, and sufficiency. It is more important for our present purposes to recall what we proposed as an important dimension of the doctrine we are investigating but to which, it appears, the existing literature has not accorded the significance it deserves. That is the fact that in the same way as the incarnation is to be seen in its full-orbed meaning as a *covenantal* incarnation, so inscripturation is again to be seen as a *covenantal* inscripturation. That conclusion is only confirmed by what has been adduced as the divine origin of the *form* as well as the *content* of Scripture.

THE CULTURAL CONTEXT OF SCRIPTURE

Much has been made in the critical literature of the impact on the human authors, and therefore on their writing of Scripture, of the cultural context in which they lived and wrote. That raises from a different perspective the question of what is to be said of the human side of Scripture. As an example of what is involved, Peter Enns has pointed the contemporary debate in that direction by his attempt to reconstruct the historical and cultural milieu of the time in which the Scriptures were written. The early chapters of Genesis and the subsequent stories of the patriarchs are prime examples of what is in view. Enns observes that "the Bible, at every turn, shows how 'connected' it is to its own world."[54] By that is meant

---

52. Ibid., 383.
53. Ibid., 435.
54. Enns, *Inspiration and Incarnation*, 20.

that "the Bible shared many of the standards, concepts, and worldviews of its ancient Near Eastern neighbors."[55] "Israel's ancient stories were composed first orally in the context of the well-established ancient Near Eastern cultures of the day," and "although the biblical stories existed earlier in oral form and only later were written down in Hebrew, one cannot argue that this oral prehistory insulated them from the influence of the ancient Near Eastern stories present in the surrounding cultures."[56] No doubt some such influence may have existed. But the question arises as to whether, then, "there is myth in the Old Testament."[57] For if, to follow Enns for the moment, the pre-biblical stories (such as the Gilgamesh story of an ancient flood) are taken to be "myth" as Enns defines it, "one might ask *why* it is that God *can't* use the category *we* call 'myth' to speak to *ancient* Israelites,"[58] with the implication in Enns' argument that God does do just that.

Enns repeatedly looks at the Old Testament through the lens of early non-biblical history and culture and finds in the latter, for example, "a helpful starting point from which to understand the origin of Israel's creation story. . . . The reason the opening chapters of Genesis look so much like the literature of ancient Mesopotamia is that the worldview categories of the ancient Near East were ubiquitous and normative at the time."[59] Or again, as to the law that was given to Israel, "we see much of the same thing. Even though Israel's law was revealed by God through Moses on Mount Sinai, these laws were by no means unique to them. It is hard to imagine that, until Mount Sinai, neither the Israelites nor the surrounding ancient Near Eastern nations had any idea that murder was wrong . . .or that one should honor one's parents."[60] Enns is here raising the question as to whether the revelation as we have it in the Old Testament is unique. His answer implies that it is not.

It is characteristic of the larger literature of which Enns' work is representative that it is frequently preoccupied with the history and culture of the times and their influence on the Bible's composition. It concludes that "when new evidence comes to light, or old evidence is seen in a new

---

55. Ibid., 46.
56. Ibid., 50–51.
57. Ibid., 49.
58. Ibid., 50.
59. Ibid., 53.
60. Ibid., 57.

Biblical Inspiration and Authority 153

light, we must be willing to engage that evidence *and adjust our doctrine accordingly.*"[61] The argument for doctrinal flexibility and instability does not sit well with the confessional statement that "the authority of the holy scripture, for which it ought to be believed and obeyed, dependeth not upon the testimony of any man or church, but wholly upon God *the author thereof.*"[62] When the conclusion is advanced that "what the Bible is must be understood in light of the cultural context in which it was given,"[63] the suggestion would seem to be implied that a certain kind of "kenoticism," or a divine emptying in the origin of Scripture, is involved in the authors' position.[64] An important relevant rejoinder is contained in the report of the Historical and Theological Field Committee of Westminster Theological Seminary which observes that "while it is appropriate and important to seek to understand biblical passages in terms of their cultural context, it is inappropriate, in a Reformed, confessional context, to let those phenomena determine what the Bible *is* (i.e., a doctrine of Scripture). Such a methodology denies that we determine our doctrine of Scripture in terms of its self-witness *alone*; it denies that a *doctrine* of Scripture is gleaned by virtue of what Scripture says about *itself.*"[65] Enns writes that "one would have to be somewhat self-absorbed to think he or she can have anything final to say on what the Bible *is* and what we should *do* with it."[66] It should be clear that such a conclusion does not accord with the *theopneustos*, or breathing out, or inspiration claimed in 2 Timothy 3:16.

If it is supposed for the sake of argument that the Bible is not unique (in the sense that Enns, for example, intends) by reason that the non-Israelitish nations as well as Israel knew that murder was wrong, the question arises as to *why* that might have been so. Why, that is to say, was the extra-Israelitish culture in that respect what it was? By reason

---

61. Ibid., 14, italics added.

62. Westminster Confession of Faith. I:4, italics added.

63. Enns, *Inspiration and Incarnation*, 41.

64. The suggestion of scriptural "kenoticism" derives from the corresponding misreading of Philippians 2:7, where the phrase translated in the KJV as "made himself of no reputation," which can be read literally in the Greek text as "emptied himself," is falsely taken to mean that in his incarnation Christ set aside, or emptied himself of, his divine glory.

65. Westminster Theological Seminary Committee Report, "*Inspiration and Incarnation.*" Online: http://www.bible-researcher.com/enns1.html.

66. Enns, *Inspiration and Incarnation*, 167.

of God's initial communication to Adam in his capacity as the federal head and representative head of the race, and by virtue of God's common grace in the years and decades that followed, there was born and preserved in the human consciousness a conception of the law of God, darkened and shadowed and indistinct though that may have become as a result of man's fallenness and sinful state. Again, the sense of God, the *sensus deitatis*, and the common knowledge of God or the residue of God-consciousness in the human soul, preserves a sense of morality, of rightness and wrongness. It is beyond our immediate context to recall that the condemnation of men in sin is that they naturally suppress every wakening awareness of God that that residual sense projects to the surface of consciousness (See Rom 1:18).

Interest attaches, in the contemporary critical literature, to the manner in which the New Testament writers made use of the Old Testament data. In that connection, Enns has made an interesting suggestion regarding the "apostolic hermeneutic." That, as he sees it, is a "christotelic" hermeneutic,[67] meaning that for the apostles "the coming of Christ is so climactic that it required [them] to look at the Old Testament in a whole new light."[68] That is, "to read the Old Testament 'christotelically' is to read it *already knowing* that Christ is somehow the *end* to which the Old Testament story is heading."[69] That is all very well. The New Testament writers were, of course, able to look at the Old Testament in such a way that, in the course of their interpretations, light was thrown on it by the knowledge they possessed of the fact that Christ in his redemptive mission had fulfilled the Old Testament promises and projections. He was the antitype of the types of the Old Testament administration of the Covenant of Grace. But it would be a serious mistake to conclude that the "christotelic hermeneutic" could be adduced to mean simply that such a new perspective, proper in itself, had been established. What is more fundamentally at issue, and what contemporary criticism is reluctant to acknowledge, is that the New Testament interpretation of Old Testament texts is, in fact, part of the original meaning of the Old Testament text as its ultimate author, the Holy Spirit, intended.[70]

67. Ibid., 154.
68. Ibid., 160.
69. Ibid., 154.

70. The point has been made by Scott in "Inspiration and Interpretation of God's Word, Part I," 172.

The question confronting us, then, is: "What are we to take as the meaning of Scripture?" Our argument to this point has relied on the fact that there does not exist an equal ultimacy between the secondary, human authors and the primary author, the Holy Spirit. That primary authorship means that an "error-preventing inspiration"[71] has informed the production of Scripture. Our task in reading the Scripture, then, is to grasp the meaning that God intended. It is not sufficient to say that the meaning of the Scripture is simply what the first hearers or readers of the text might have understood it to mean. Nor it is adequate to say that the meaning is confined or restricted to what the human authors understood by what they were writing. The meaning of Scripture is what its ultimate author, the Holy Spirit, intended to convey by it. And the human authors cannot be said necessarily to have held in mind all that God the Holy Spirit intended.[72]

As to the question of the proper methods of interpretation, much is to be said for the careful application of the so-called grammatical-historical method. In that, attention is paid not only to the linguistic structure of the text but to the historical situation in which the human writers produced their work, under what we have seen as the supervising inspiration of the Holy Spirit. But such a grammatical-historical procedure is to be seen as providing only a first approximation to God's intended meaning. That is to be grasped in the light of the full revelation that God has made in the Scriptures and in the light of the divinely ordered consistency that exists in the Scriptures in all their parts. That means, in other words, that attention is to be paid, in the interpretation of Scripture, to what has been called the analogy of faith, or the analogy of Scripture. Scripture, that is, is its own interpreter.

We recall, finally, Warfield's caution that there *is* in the case of Christ's incarnation, but there *is not* in the case of the Scriptures, a hypostatic union of the divine and the human. We have seen it implied that in the case of both incarnation and inscripturation the divine is *essential* and the human is *contingent,* though real. It is in the light of that realization that we have accorded priority to the Holy Spirit as the author of Scripture. That, we have said, establishes its inspiration and authority.

---

71. Ibid., 158.
72. For a valuable discussion of the meaning of Scripture see ibid., 168–174.

CONCLUSION

We recall by way of summary our evaluation of Scripture on which our entire argument regarding the meaning and the message of the cross of Christ stands. The Bible *is* the Word of God. It is the speech of God to us in our state of sin. God, in the Person of his Holy Spirit, is its author. Further, we understand the Bible to be the Word of God because it is self-attesting as to its scripturicity, inspiration, and authority. The full persuasion to that effect turns, on the level of our Spirit-induced apprehension of its truth, on the awareness that the inscripturation of God's revelation is a covenantal inscripturation. God, moreover, has accommodated his speech to us to our sinful condition. His inscripturated Word, as is to be said of all of his revelation, is anthropomorphic. We can see a legitimate analogy between inscripturation and incarnation, in that the divine-human natures in Christ are reflected in the divine-human nature of Scripture. That analogy holds while at the same time it is realized that the hypostatic union of the divine and human natures in Christ is not, and of course cannot be, precisely reflected in the same sense in the Scriptures. Finally, when we say that our doctrine of Scripture, of what the Scripture is and what it means, is determined by the Scripture's self-attestation and what it says of itself, we reject the claim that it is flexibly determined by any external cultural or evidential data. By the internal testimony of the Spirit, who in the grace of regeneration takes away the darkness of soul and enables us to see what was always there to be seen, and by the grace of illumination with which he blesses our journey, we know that the Scriptures are the Word of God because in them we hear God speaking. We know that the Scriptures are inerrant and infallible by reason that God who is their author is a God of truth. The meaning of the Scripture is the meaning that God intended, and it does not depend simply or only on human authorial intent or what it might have meant to original readers or hearers.

The Scripture as given, then, is the only rule of life and belief.

Bibliography

Alexander, Cecil Frances. *There Is a Green Hill Far Away*. In *Trinity Hymnal*, 256. Atlanta: Great Commissions Publications, Revised edition, 1990.

Anonymous. *O Christ, in Thee my soul has found*. Online: http://www.sermonaudio.com/hymn_details.asp?PID=nonebutchristcansatisfy.

Auber, Harriet. *Our blest Redeemer, ere He breathed His tender, last farewell*. In *Congregational Praise*, 209. London: Independent Press, for the Congregational Union of England and Wales, 1951.

Bahnsen, Greg L. *Van Til's Apologetics: Readings and Analysis*. Phillipsburg, NJ: P&R, 1998.

Barker, W. S. Review of *The Authority and Interpretation of the Bible: An Historical Approach*, by Jack Rogers and Donald McKim. *Presbyterion* 6 (1980) 96–107.

Bavinck, Herman. *Reformed Dogmatics. Volume 1: Prolegomena*. Edited by John Bolt. Translated by John Vriend. Grand Rapids: Baker, 2003.

———. *Reformed Dogmatics. Volume 3: Sin and Salvation in Christ*. Edited by John Bolt. Translated by John Vriend. Grand Rapids: Baker, 2006.

Berkhof, Louis. *Systematic Theology*. Grand Rapids: Eerdmans, 1939.

———. *Systematic Theology*. New Edition. Introductory Volume. Grand Rapids: Eerdmans, 1996.

Blanchard, John. *Does God believe in atheists?* Darlington, UK: Evangelical Press, 2000.

Bridges, Jerry and Bob Bevington. *The Bookends of the Christian Life*. Wheaton, IL: Crossway, 2009.

Brown, John. *An Exposition of the Epistle of Paul the Apostle to the Galatians*. Minneapolis: Klock & Klock, 1981.

Calvin, John. *Commentaries*. 22 vols. Grand Rapids: Baker, 1979.

———. *Institutes of the Christian Religion*. Edited by John T. McNeill. Translated by Ford Lewis Battles. 2 vols. Philadelphia: Westminster, 1960.

Candlish, Robert. *A Commentary on 1 John*. London: Banner of Truth, 1973.

Carson, D. A. *The Gagging of God: Christianity Confronts Pluralism*. Grand Rapids: Zondervan, 1996.

Charnock, Stephen. *The Existence and Attributes of God*. Minneapolis: Klock & Klock, 1977.

Congregational Praise (hymnal). London: Independent Press, for the Congregational Union of England and Wales, 1951.

Cowper, William. *There Is a Fountain Filled with Blood*. In *Trinity Hymnal*, 253, and various hymnals.

Cunningham, William. *Historical Theology*. 2 vols. London: Banner of Truth, 1960.

Dabney, Robert L. *Discussions: Evangelical and Theological*. Vol. 1. London: Banner of Truth, 1967.

Davidson, Robert and A. R. C. Leaney. *Biblical Criticism: The Pelican Guide to Modern Theology.* Vol. 3. Harmondsworth, UK: Penguin, 1970.

Descartes, René. *Discourse on Method and the Meditations on First Philosophy.* Translated by Donald A. Cress. Indianapolis, IN: Hackett, 1998.

Edwards, Jonathan. *The Freedom of the Will.* Morgan, PA: Soli Deo Gloria, 1996.

Elliott, Paul M. *Christianity and Neo-Liberalism: The Spiritual Crisis in the Orthodox Presbyterian Church and Beyond.* Unicoi, TN: Trinity Foundation, 2005.

Enns, Peter. *Inspiration and Incarnation: Evangelicals and the Problem of the Old Testament.* Grand Rapids: Baker, 2005.

———. "Interaction with Bruce Waltke." *Westminster Theological Journal* 71, 1 (2009) 97–114.

Ferguson, Sinclair. *John Owen on the Christian Life.* Edinburgh: Banner of Truth, 1987.

Gaffin, Richard B. Jr. *By Faith, Not By Sight.* Milton Keynes, UK: Paternoster, 2006.

———. *God's Word in Servant Form: Abraham Kuyper and Herman Bavinck on the Doctrine of Scripture.* Jackson, MS: Reformed Academic, 2008.

———. "Paul the Theologian." *Westminster Theological Journal* 62, 1 (2000) 121–41.

———. *Resurrection and Redemption: A Study in Paul's Soteriology.* Phillipsburg, NJ: P&R, 1987.

Godfrey, W. R. Review of *The Authority and Interpretation of the Bible: An Historical Approach*, by Jack Rogers and Donald McKim. *Christianity Today* 25/9 (May 8, 1981) 59.

Hanson, R. P. C. Introduction. In Robert Davidson and A. R. C. Leaney. *Biblical Criticism. The Pelican Guide to Modern Theology.* Vol. 3. Harmondsworth, UK: Penguin, 1970.

Harnack, Adolf. *History of Dogma.* 7 vols. Translated by James Millar. New York: Dover, 1951.

———. *Outlines of the History of Dogma.* Translated by E. K. Mitchell. Boston: Beacon, 1957.

Hebert, Gabriel. *Fundamentalism and the Church of God.* London: S.C.M., 1957.

Hendriksen, William. *New Testament Commentary: Exposition of the Gospel According to John.* 2 vols. Grand Rapids: Baker, 1954.

Hodge, Alexander A. and Benjamin B. Warfield. *Inspiration.* Grand Rapids: Baker, 1979.

Hodge, Charles. *A Commentary on 1 & 2 Corinthians.* Edinburgh: Banner of Truth, 1974.

Hughes, Philip Edgcumbe. *A Commentary on the Epistle to the Hebrews.* Grand Rapids: Eerdmans, 1977.

———. *Paul's Second Epistle to the Corinthians.* Grand Rapids: Eerdmans, 1962.

Kant, Immanuel. *Critique of Pure Reason.* Translated by F. Max Miller. New York: Macmillan, 1966.

Kelly, Douglas F. *Systematic Theology. Volume One: Grounded in Holy Scripture and understood in the light of the Church.* Fearn, Scotland: Christian Focus, Mentor Imprint, 2008.

Kuyper, Abraham. *Principles of Sacred Theology.* Translated by J. Hendrik De Vries. Grand Rapids: Eerdmans, 1963.

———. *The Work of the Holy Spirit.* Translated by Henri De Vries. Grand Rapids: Eerdmans, 1956.

Lindsell, Harold. *The Battle for the Bible.* Grand Rapids: Zondervan, 1976.

Lloyd-Jones, D. Martyn. *The cross*. Westchester, IL: Crossway, 1986.
———. *The Cross: The Vindication of God*. London: Banner of Truth, n.d.
Martin, Robert P. *Accuracy of Translation and the New International Version: The Primary Criterion in Evaluating Bible Versions*. Edinburgh: Banner of Truth, 1989.
Muller, Richard A. *Post-Reformation Reformed Dogmatics. Volume 2: Holy Scripture: The Cognitive Foundation of Theology*. Grand Rapids: Baker, 2003.
Murray, John. *Calvin on Scripture and Divine Sovereignty*. Grand Rapids: Baker, 1960.
———. *Collected Writings of John Murray*. 4 vols. Edinburgh: Banner of Truth, 1976-82.
———. "Definitive Sanctification." In *Collected Writings of John Murray*. Vol. 2, 277-84. Edinburgh: Banner of Truth, 1977.
———. *Principles of Conduct: Aspects of Biblical Ethics*. Grand Rapids: Eerdmans, 1957.
———. "Progressive Sanctification." In *Collected Writings of John Murray*. Vol. 2, 294-304. Edinburgh: Banner of Truth, 1977.
———. *Redemption - Accomplished and Applied*. Grand Rapids: Eerdmans, 1955.
———. "The Attestation of Scripture." In N. B. Stonehouse and Paul Woolley, eds. *The Infallible Word*. 1-52. Grand Rapids: Eerdmans, 1946.
———. *The Epistle to the Romans*. Vol. 1. Grand Rapids: Eerdmans, 1959.
———. "The Holy Scriptures." In *Collected Writings of John Murray*. Vol. 1, 1-26. Edinburgh: Banner of Truth, 1976.
Murray, John and Ned B. Stonehouse. *The Free Offer of the Gospel*: A report to the Fifteenth General Assembly of the Orthodox Presbyterian Church, 1948. Phillipsburg, NJ: Lewis J. Grotenhuis, n.d. Also reprinted in John Murray. *Collected Writings of John Murray*. Vol. 4, 113-32. Edinburgh: Banner of Truth, 1982.
Newton, John. *Approach, My Soul, the Mercy Seat*. In *Trinity Hymnal*, 507. Atlanta: Great Commissions Publications, Revised edition, 1990.
Owen, John. *Christologia: The Person of Christ—God and Man*. In *The Works of John Owen*. Edited by William H. Goold, 1850-53. Vol. 1, 1-272. London: Banner of Truth, 1965.
———. *Discourse Concerning the Holy Spirit*. In *The Works of John Owen*. Edited by William H. Goold, 1850-53. Vol. 3. London: Banner of Truth, 1965.
———. "The causes, ways, and means of understanding the mind of God as revealed in his word, with assurance therein." In *The Works of John Owen*. Vol. 4, 118-234. London: Banner of Truth, 1967.
Packer, James I. *Beyond the Battle for the Bible*. Westchester, IL: Cornerstone, 1980.
———. *'Fundamentalism' and the Word of God: Some Evangelical Principles*. Grand Rapids: Eerdmans, 1958.
Peterson, Robert A. *Calvin and the Atonement*. Fearn, Scotland: Christian Focus, Mentor Imprint, 1999.
———. *Calvin's Doctrine of the Atonement*. Phillipsburg, NJ: Presbyterian and Reformed, 1983.
Pink, Arthur W. *The Satisfaction of Christ*. Grand Rapids: Zondervan, 1955.
Reymond, Robert L. *A New Systematic Theology of the Christian Faith*. Nashville: Nelson, 1998.
Rogers, Jack and Donald McKim. *The Authority and Interpretation of the Bible: An Historical Approach*. San Francisco: Harper & Row, 1979.
Savoy Declaration of Faith. 1658. Various editions.

Scott, James W. "The Inspiration and Interpretation of God's Word, with special reference to Peter Enns. Part I. Inspiration and its Implications." *Westminster Theological Journal* 71, 1 (2009) 129–83.

———. "The Inspiration and Interpretation of God's Word, with special reference to Peter Enns. Part II. The Interpretation of Representative Passages." *Westminster Theological Journal* 71, 2 (2009) 247–79.

Scougal, Henry. *The Life of God in the Soul of Man*. Harrisonburg: Sprinkle, 1986.

Second London (Baptist) Confession. 1689. Various editions.

Shedd, W. G. T. *A History of Christian Doctrine*. 2 vols. New York: Scribners, 1868.

———. *Dogmatic Theology*. 3 vols. Grand Rapids: Zondervan, n.d.

Shepherd, Norman. *The Call of Grace: How the Covenant Illuminates Salvation and Evangelism*. Phillipsburg, NJ: P&R, 2000.

Sproul, R. C. *Faith Alone: The Evangelical Doctrine of Justification*. Grand Rapids: Baker, 1995.

———. *Grace Unknown: The Heart of Reformed Theology*. Grand Rapids: Baker, 1997.

Stonehouse, N. B., and Paul Woolley. *The Infallible Word: A Symposium by the members of the Faculty of Westminster Theological Seminary*. Grand Rapids: Eerdmans, 1946.

Toplady, Augustus, M. *Rock of Ages, Cleft for Me*. In *Trinity Hymnal*, 499, and various hymnals.

Trinity Hymnal. Atlanta: Great Commissions Publications, Revised edition, 1990.

Trueman, Carl. *Minority Report: Unpopular Thought on Everything from Ancient Christianity to Zen-Calvinism*. Fearn, Scotland: Christian Focus, Mentor Imprint, 2008.

Turretin, Francis. *Institutes of Elenctic Theology*. Vol. 1. Translated by George Musgrave Giger. Edited by James T. Dennison. Phillipsburg, NJ: P&R, 1992.

———. *Institutes of Elenctic Theology*. Vol. 2. Translated by George Musgrave Giger. Edited by James T. Dennison. Phillipsburg, NJ: P&R, 1994.

Van Til, Cornelius. *A Christian Theory of Knowledge*. Philadelphia: Presbyterian and Reformed, 1969.

———. *The Defense of the Faith*. Philadelphia: Presbyterian and Reformed, 1963.

Vickers, Douglas. *Christian Confession and the Crackling Thorn*. Grand Rapids: Reformation Heritage Books, 2004.

———. *Divine Redemption and the Refuge of Faith*. Grand Rapids: Reformation Heritage Books, 2005.

———. *The Bondage of Grace*. Philadelphia: Skilton House, 1997.

———. *The Fracture of Faith: Recovering belief of the gospel in a postmodern world*. Fearn, Scotland: Christian Focus, Mentor Imprint. 2000.

———. *The Immediacy of God*. Eugene, OR: Wipf & Stock, 2009.

———. *When God Converts a Sinner*. Eugene, OR: Wipf & Stock, 2008.

Vos, Geerhardus. *Biblical Theology: Old and New Testaments*. Grand Rapids: Eerdmans, 1948.

Waltke, Bruce. K. *An Old Testament Theology: an exegetical, canonical, and thematic approach*. Grand Rapids: Zondervan, 2007.

———. "Response: Interaction with Peter Enns." *Westminster Theological Journal* 71, 1 (2009) 115–28.

———. "Revisiting *Inspiration and Incarnation*." *Westminster Theological Journal* 71, 1 (2009) 83–95.

Warfield, Benjamin B. *Calvin and Calvinism*. Grand Rapids: Baker, 2003.

———. "Calvin's Doctrine of the Knowledge of God." In *Calvin and Augustine*. Philadelphia: Presbyterian and Reformed, 1971, 29–130.

———. *The Inspiration and Authority of the Bible*. Philadelphia: Presbyterian and Reformed, 1967.

Watts, Isaac. *When I Survey the Wondrous Cross*. In *Trinity Hymnal*, 252. Atlanta: Great Commissions Publications, Revised edition, 1990.

Weatherhead, Leslie. *A Plain Man Looks at the Cross*. New York: Abingdon-Cokesbury, 1945.

Wells, D. F. Review of *The Authority and Interpretation of the Bible: An Historical Approach*, by Jack Rogers and Donald McKim. *Westminster Theological Journal* 43 (1980–81) 152–55.

Westminster Confession of Faith, 1647. Various editions.

Westminster Shorter Catechism. 1647. Various editions.

Westminster Theological Seminary Historical and Theological Field Committee. "*Inspiration and Incarnation*: A Response." April 4, 2006. No pages. Online: http://www.bible-researcher.com/enns1.html.

Woodbridge, John D. *Biblical Authority: A Critique of the Rogers/McKim Proposal*. Grand Rapids: Zondervan, 1982.

———. Review of *The Authority and Interpretation of the Bible: An Historical Approach*, by Jack Rogers and Donald McKim. *Trinity Journal* NS 1 (1980) 165–236.

Wright, N. T. *What Saint Paul Really Said: Was Paul of Tarsus the real founder of Christianity?* Grand Rapids: Eerdmans, 1997.

Young, Edward J. *Thy Word is Truth*. Grand Rapids: Eerdmans, 1957.

www.ingramcontent.com/pod-product-compliance
Lightning Source LLC
Chambersburg PA
CBHW051938160426
43198CB00013B/2212